Christian Missions in
ANDHRA

Dr. Sandeep K. Dasari

INDIA · SINGAPORE · MALAYSIA

ISBN
Paperback 979-8-89519-552-9
Hardcase 979-8-89588-948-0

DEDICATION

To my beloved mother, Savithri Venkata Reddy Dasari, whose love, strength, and unwavering faith continue to inspire me every day. Your spirit lives on in every page of this work, guiding me through every step of this journey. This book is a tribute to your memory and the light you brought into my life.

CONTENTS

PREFACE

This study is an examination of Christian Missionaries and their activities in Guntur and its surroundings in Krishna district during 19th century.

Until 1859 there was a Guntur district with its headquarters at Guntur. It consisted of the revenue sub divisions of Guntur, Tenali, Narsaraopet and Ongole. In 1858 it was abolished and divided between the districts of Rajahmundry and Machilipatnam, which were renamed as Godavari and Krishna Districts. The present day Guntur District was created in 1904 out of Ongole taluq of Nellore and portions by Krishna District. In Guntur Region Christian Missionary Enterprise has a long history.

The context of European revivalism forms the back drop within which Christian Missionaries came to India. In this study the relations between the East India Company and the missionaries in India, during the period of 1783 to 1813 are discussed. With the passing of the Charter Act 1813 by the Britlsh Parliament, colonial and political interests in and been encouraging the missionary movement. What was the stand of the missionaries in this regard?

Christian Missionary activity is the history of the missionaries in South India and expansion of various missions in the Telugu speaking areas which have been reconstructed.

Considerable attention has also been focused on socio-economic methods and vehicle employed by the missionaries in their proselytisation work. Prior to 18th century the converts were from higher castes. During the 18th century, the focus of conversions was the lower castes. Mass-conversion of lower castes was a significant phenomenon of the 19th century. What were the factors which impelled such large scale conversions?

Any study of Christianity in India must examine the question of caste in the Church. How did the missionaries perceive caste? Did they adopt any strategies to eradicate caste in the Church or was it accommodated within the Church?

The social activities and contributions of the missionaries in the fields of education and health have also been examined and finally, the linkages between the Christian Missionary activity and no social reform and national consciousness have also been explored.

The prominent books for the study of Christianity in India in general are K. Ingham, Reformers in India (1956); D.B. Forester, Caste and Christianity (1980); D.A. Oddie, Social Protest in India (1981); W.J. Picket, Christian Mass Movements in India (1937); Laldeens, Christian Missionaries and Colonialism (1988); W.R. Smith, The Indirect Effects of Christian Missionaries (1928); M.A. Sherring, The History of Protestant Missions in India, 1707-1881 (1884); Julias Ritcher, A History of Missions in India (1908); Stephen Neil, The Story of Christian Church in India and Pakistan J.A. Sharrock South Indian Mission (1910); J. Hough, A History of Christianity in India, C.B. Fifth, An Introduction to Indian Church History (1981); V.S. Azaraiah, Indian and Christian Movement (1938); P. Thomas, Christians and Christianity in India and Pakistan (1954).

Telugu Christian Missionaries working in the Telugu speaking area have written extensively on their work. To cite a view M.L. Dolbeer, A History of Lutheranism in Andhra Desa 1842-1920 (1959), and also Andhra Evangelical Lutheran Church Brief History (1950); C.H. Swavely, One Hundred Years in the Telugu Country 1842-1942 (1952); Drack and Kuder, The Telugu Mission (1914); Glad Stone, The Church Missionary Society in Telugu Country (1914); E.S. Bromley, They men sent from God (1937); Herbertware,

Christian Missions in Telugu Country (1941); A.T. Fishman, For this Purpose (1941), give us a complete history of Christian Missions in Andhra.

Besides these, the study has drawn heavily on the correspondence of the father Heyer Life and Letters of Father C.F. Heyer own story, reports of Missionary Conferences, Minutes of Andhra Christian Council, District Gazetteers and Census Reports. In addition a wide range of Missionary Journals like Harvest Field, East and West, Indian Evangelical Review, Gospel Witness, Christian Missionary Intelligencer, Indian Church Quarterly Review, Indian Church History Review have also been consulted.

CHAPTER-1
MISSIONS OF SOUTH INDIA

The spread of Christianity in India started with arrival of St. Thomas, the first Disciple of Jesus Christ. Thomas arrived from Persia in 53 A.D.[1]. He started his proselytizing work from the South Indian Malabar Coastal area, in Cranganore.

He converted some families namely Kali, Kalayankar, Shankarapurru, and Pakalomottam who were the most important among Palur Community. Thomas moved to Malayam Kara, Palayar, Koka Manngalam, Nirannaman, Chanyas, Kilwalh where he established Christian Societies. Commercial contracts between South India and the ports of Roman Empire even prior to the Christian era were frequent. One could surmise that it would have been difficult for the saint to land in a port of Malabar[3]. After Thomas, Christians of the Malabar coast visited East Syris. Mesapotomia and Persian countries. Christians visited India from these regions as well, there was a constant contact between the two[4].

Next Bishop Thomas arrived from Edesa in 345 A.D. to the Malabar Coast. With his arrival Christians strengthened themselves in South India. These religious contacts with Syria were further strengthened because of trade links. These converts were called Syrian Christians to be distinguished from Thomas Christians who were earlier converts[5]. Apart from these two Roman Catholics in India as early as the 14th Century[6], Evidence of the 16th century reveal that the Catholic communities were living near Cape Camorin[7]. A Christian Community existed on the South West Coast of India long before the arrival of European in the middle of the 16th century[8]. At this time Europeans whose primary interest was trade, also brought with them missionaries who became active in the Indian soil. For example the Portuguese, who were Catholics encouraged missionary activities[9].

The 18th century was significant in the history of Christianity in India. At this time, the Europeans started to gain control over trade throughout the sub-continent. The Portuguese Catholics were the first to enter the Indian scene[10]. They were followed by Italians and other European catholic missionaries[11].

In South India, the southern districts have been long strong holds of Catholic Christianity[12]. For instance, St. Francis Xavier arrived in Goa on May 16th 1542, later Nobili (1606), the founder of Madhurai Mission, Besschi, Schultz, Janickie are prominent names associated with the rising of the Christian Church in South India[13]. The English missionary activity was closely linked with the Evangelical movement. The social and religious conditions in 18th century England were absolutely deplorable. It was felt that there was serious decline in moral standards and the Church also showed a lack of spirituality and social involvement. Against this background a religious revival movement emerged with leaders like John Wesley and White Field, two prominent Methodists. This revivals movement was marked by a strong belief in the saving power of the Christian Gospel and also in the necessity of personal conversion and an intense moral earnestness[14]. The revival stammed from the overall socio-economic changes and spiritual bankruptcy which swept the decadent English Society[15].

In the pre-industrial period, the relations between aristocracy and working class was to some extent based on a certain degree of reciprocal support. But consequent upon the industrial revolution, society, social relations and values changed. Crowding in cities, the dismal conditions of the life and work of the labouring classes, the dominance of money, market and profit, all combined to create much cultural, psychological and moral depression among the working class[16].

It was among the depressed working class that the revivalist movement found its great adherents. The movement was in a way the product of advancing industrialism and of the emergence of a new ethic for a new society[17]. The basic conception of revivalism was to generate the spread of new enthusiasm and intense moral earnestness coupled with a deep concern for the unsaved. For example a deep concern for the salvation of the non-Christians in other countries, unprivileged poor, which manifested itself in a large number of charitable activities like establishing schools and hospitals and distributing charitable tracts. In social terms the movement was very much "middle class" in character and it spread widely among the trading and professional class[18].

As a result, many foreign missionary societies were formed with a view of advancing their faith in distant countries. They looked upon the missionaries in foreign country with a romantic spiritual vision and adventurism[19]. Missionaries followed close on heels of colonial powers. The Jesuit Missionaries and to be more specific Francis Xavier did indeed come as a royal missionary. But the missionary zeal which spread Christianity all over the world in most cases was sponsored by the colonial power[20]. Lal Deena in his work Christian Missions and Colonialism suggest, in most cases the missionaries selfless work among people tended to legitimate the colonial occupation[21]. The revivalist trends were to strongly influence East Indian Company policies regarding missionary activities in the colonies especially in India. East India Company, with the assumption of political power in 1757 after the battle of Plassey maintained a policy of strict neutrality[22]. Missionaries were refused entry in to the East India Company territories during the late 18th and early 19th centuries. The Company followed a general policy of non-interference in social affairs and social organization of the Indians. Their desire was to maintain peaceful conditions in which the East India Company could work and their trade could prosper. Since their major interest was to protest their trade, they did not want anything to endanger that interest[23].

In 1806 the Vellore mutiny broke out. A major reason for the mutiny was that the Madras Government for the sake of uniformity, had required Indian sepoy troops, to wear a new kind of turban and remove their distinguishing caste marks and earrings when on parade. The sepoys suspected this order as an attempt to convert them into Christianity and they revolved[24]. This mutiny at Vellore confirmed the Company's belief of their soundness of policy of neutrality. On the other hand, there were chaplains of the Company, such as the famous Henry Martin, who took a great interest in the promotion of missionary work among Indians even while the Company government violently opposed the missionaries[25].

The turn of the 18th century brought keener consciousness among the Christian Churches in England as to the obligation of the British Government to bring education, religious and moral advancement to the people under their rule[26]. In 1793 on the eve of the renewal of the Company's charter, the debate on the missionaries entrance into India was once again started[27].

The prominent evangelical social reformer, Wilberforce argued that the Company should accept the responsibility for promoting the spiritual welfare of its Indian subjects and that school masters and chaplains should be sent out to work among them. This was opposed by the Directors of the Company in the British Parliament[28]. The Directors argued that interference with the beliefs of the people of India would create dissatisfaction and Jeopardize British interests and hence the Company was opposing the entry of missionaries into India[29]. Wilberforce on his part vociferously argued that the whole justification and control over India lay in the christianisation of the Indian people[30]. On the same lines, Fr. Claudius Buchanan, then Provost of the College of Fort William, also found no other way than Christianizing India for establishing unbreakable friendship between Indians and Britishers. Charles Grant, an influential East India Company Director, was an evangelist. He advocated a pro-missionary stand. He argued that obristian missionaries and their work would give a political stability to the Company a rule. Conversions would make legitimate the control of the Indians for ever by British Government[31]. Wilberforce appealed to his country men that they should do their best to strike roots in Indian soil by transplanting their principles, laws, institutions and manners above all the religion and morals[32]. He argued that this would ensure the permanent subjection of India to British rule, sentiments that were echoed and shared by Charles Grant[33].

At last the 1813 Charter Act, the British Parliament removed all restrictions on missionary activities. Clause-XXXII of the Charter Act of 1813 allowed the freedom for propagating Christianity[34]. With this the missionary movement entered into a crucial phase. The Charter Act also provided one lakh of Rupees from the Indian revenue for education, revival of the own learning of Indian and western science among the inhabitants of the British territories in India, which proved critical in advancing missionary work[35].

Missions from the European continent, most of those from the United States of America came after the 1813 Charter Act removed the restrictions which had operated against non-British Missionary Societies[36].

The 1833 Charter Act further lifted all restrictions on the entry of missionaries into India[37]. From the 19th century, the churches in Europe, Great Britain, Australia, United States of America and Canada were moved and inspired by the holy spirit of evangelizing the world. The churches formed into societies. The first mission society was formed in England, the Society for Promoting Christian Knowledge (S.P.C.K.) in 1698, followed by the Society for Propagation of the Gospel in Foreign Parts (Sept..) in 1701[38]. The Baptist Missionary Society was formed in 1792 by William Carey (1781-1834). Others were, the London Missionary society in 1795, The Religious Tract Society in 1799 in Britain, British Foreign missions Society in 1804, The American Bible Society in 1816, American Baptist Missionary union in 1816, American Baptist Mission Society in 1876[39]. In the early history of Evangelical Lutheran church in American, two dates, a century aparty, are significant, 1742 the landing of a American church missionary Melchior Muhlen berg, on the shore of the Western hemisphere, the other 1842 whom the first, American Luther foreign mission in India was established by John Christian Fedrick Heyer in Guntur, Andhra[40].

The first protestant missionary activity in south India was in the Danish settlement of Tranquebar, king Fedrick IV (1699-1730) of Denmark sponsored the first protestant mission work in India, sending German pietists, Bartholomew Ziegenbalg (1683-1719), and Henry Plutsschau (1678-1747) from the Frankean institutions at Halle, to Tranquebar[41]. The Dutch East India company also sent their missionaries to Palakoullu area in Andhra region.

Missions and their work were affected by the ups and downs of Anglo-French rivalry. The war of the Austrian succession, in Europe, in which French and English took opposite sides, spread to India, and even after the treaty of Aix-la-chapelle in 1748 continued in India through the intrigues of the French to gain control over the Nawab of Carnatic and Nizam of Hyderabad[42]. The Northern Circars was given to French in 1753 in return for training the Nizam's army. In 1765 the English took over the Northern Circars with the defeat of the French troops, and suspended the Jesuit order in 1773[43].

With the decline of Portuguese power and therefore of Roman Catholics, the Protestants used the opportunity to convert large numbers into their fold mainly from the lower classes. A number of missionary societies took interest in propagating the Protestant faith in South India. Protestant missionary work in South India began in Kerala during the first decade of the 19th century. William Tobias Ringiltaube began his work in the southern parts or Kerala in 1806. Though he was not granted permission to reside there, in 1806 after acceptance of the British supremacy by the local governments. He was given a permission to start a society in 1809. Thus the work of London Missionary Society (L.M.S) in the southern part of Kerala was started. In 1816 the Church Missionary Society (C.M.S) also commenced its work in Kerala. The C.M.S. was in fact invited by Co.Munro, the British resident in Travancore and Cochin. The work of C.M.S. was mainly in the central part of Kerala[44]. In 1834, the Baseil Evangelical Missionary society commenced its work in the northern parts of Kerala[45]. Madras became the focus of Church Missionary Society work as early as 1814.

The 18th century Lutheran Mission based on the Danish settlement of Tranquebar, founded by Ziegenbalgh was the first to preach to the Hindus of Madras Ziegenbagh's work was carried on by Benjamin Schultz from 1750 to 1798 in Madras, Trichinopoly and Tinnevally. In 1826 Society for Propagation of Gospel followed to Madras. The chief centres of the Society for Propagation Gospel were Trichinopoly. Tanjore, Tinnevelly and Madurai[46]. Other societies were the Methodist Missionary Society in Mysore and Hyderabad, The Baseil Mission in South Kerala and North Malabar, The Church of Scotland Mission in and near Madras city and The Salvation Army in Kerala[47].

The spread of Christianity in India was due to the revival movement in Britain. The Societies primary motive was to save the unsaved people all over the world, it further imbread them with a civilizing mission. The policy of the colonial governments in India changing with the time for instance the Dutch, French East India Companies encouraged the missionaries to spread Christianity however the changing atmosphere, and their fortunes in India, especially after defeating the French troops affected the missions as well. The maximum stations in India now was within the area conquered by the English. The latter immediately suspended the Jesuit missionary enterprise, with the end of French and Dutch power in India more or less the Roman Catholic power and activity was also on the decline and Protestantism was strenghtened.

Withe the available evidence examined in this chapter one comes to conclusion that the spread of Christianity in Indian was indirectly the result of the religious revival movement in Britain. The primary motive of these christian missionaries was to save the "Unsaved People" all over the world. The policy of setting up various missionary activities in India changed according to the government that ruled it. For instance, in the early 17th and 18th centuries the Dutch and French East India Companies encouraged missionaries to establish catholic faith but in the succeeding decades, the English rapidly gained not only political power over the Indian sub-continent but also encouraged Protestant faith.

REFERENCES

1. **Imperial Gazetteer of India**, Vol.VI, London, 1888, P.229

2. P.Thomas, **Christian** and **Christianity in India and Pakistan**, London, 1954, P.153.

3   **Gazetteer of India**, Vol.I, 1981, P.488.

4. G. Krupachari, **Telugu Sahityaniki Kristavula Seva**, Hyderabad, 1980, P.15.

5. Ibid., P.18.

6. **Gazetteer of India**, Country and People, Vol.I, P.448.

7. M.Zachariah : Christian Education and Transformation in India, C.L.S., Madras, P.12.

8. **Census of India**, 1871, Vol.XIII, Madras, P.63, and **Gazetteer of India** - Country and People, Vol.I, P.88.

9. M.Zachariah, Christian Education in India, C.L.S., Madras, P.12.

10. Vider R.Alec, **The Church in an Age of Revolution 1789 to Present Day**, Penguin, London, 1965, P.12. Also Wiebe D. Paul, **Christians in Andhra Pradesh the Minorities of Mahaboobnagar,** C.L.S., Madras, 1987, P.10. Fedrick V. Moore, **Christians in India**, 1984, Firadabad, P.11

11. Wilble D. Paul, Op.Cit., P.10.

12. Ibid.

13. Stephen Martin, **Christian Communities in Indian Context with Special Reference to Andhra Christians around Tirupati**, S.V. University, Tirupati, 1988, P.12 (Unpublished M.Phil. dissertation).

14. **Imperial Gazetteer of India**, London, 1886, P.25.

15. P. Sengupta, The Christian Missionaries in Bengal, P.1.

16. E.J. Hobsbawn, **Laboring Men**, London, 1984, Pp. 23-33. Cited in Laldeena, **Christian Missionaries and Colonialism**, Shillong, 1988, P.13

17. Laldeena, **Christian Missionaries and Colonialism**, Shillong, 1988, P.13 and Eric Strokes, **The English Utilitarians and India**, Oxford, 1979, P.29.

18. Sengupta, Op.Cit., P.12.

19. Lal Deena, Op.Cit., P.12.

20. Ibid, P.3.

21. Ibid.

22. Arthur Mathew, **Christianity and Government of India 1600-1920**, London, 1929, P.50.

23. Arthur Mathew, **Christianity and Government of India 1600-1920**, London, 1929, P.50.

24. Kenneth Ingham, Op.Cit., P.24.

25. B.B. Misra, **Indian Middle Classes, the Growth of Modern Times,** P.195, also K. Ingham, Op.Cit., P.9-10.

26. M.L. Dolbeer, **The History of the Lutheranism in Andhra Desa**, New York, 1959, P.88.

27. Ibid.

28. C.B. Firth, An Introduction to the Indian Church History, C.L.S., Madras, P.143.

29. Ibid., P.143.

30. Laldeena, Op.Cit., P.18.

31. Ibid., Pp.15-17.

32. Ibid., P.18., M.E. Gibbs, **The Anglican Church in Indian 1600-1970**, Delhi, 1972, P.50, Firth, Op.Cit., P.154., Ingham, Preface.

33. Ibid., P.17.

34. C.B. Firth, Op.Cit., P.154.

35. Ibid., P.124.

36. Chopra, **Christianity in South India**, P.232.

37. G.A. Oddie, **Social Protest in India**, Delhi, 1981, P.231.

38. Senftleben Martin, **Christian Communities**, P.13.

39. Gladstone, **The C.M.S. Telugu Mission**, Mysore, 1949, P.23.

40.   Drach and Kudler, **The Telugu Mission,**, Op.Cit., P.11.

41.   C.H. Swavely, Life and Letters of John Christian Fedrick Heyer, M.D. **Gospel Witness**, 1940, P.349.

42.   Rawlison, **A Concise History of Indian People**, 1950, P.254.

43.   M.L. Dolbeer, **The History of Lutheranism**, Op.Cit., P.35.

44.   J.W. Gladstone, Christian Missionaries Work and Socio-religious Movements in Kerala, 1850-1910, **I.C.H.R.,** June 1986, P.30, also Gladstone, **South India**, Op.Cit., P.48.

CHAPTER-2
CHRISTIAN MISSIONS IN ANDHRA

In this chapter the major discussion is on various missions which belonged to different countries. A brief historical narration follows about the missions in the Telugu speaking area. A special focus is on four important missionary societies, American Lutheran Mission, Baptist Missionary Society, London Missionary Society and Church Missionary Society. A special reference is made to the Guntur region which was a part of the Krishna District upto the beginning of the present century. Another significant point that has been highlighted is that the strengthening of the protestant missionaries activity was not only by the East India Company, but also by District Collectors and noteworthy officials who individually and in their official capacities helped the missionaries financially and otherwise.

At the end of the 16th century, Jesuits established Christianity in the capital cities of the Raya of Vijayanagara, Chandragiri and Vellore in Andhra. The next attempt to preach in Andhra was made by the Theatines and Augustinians with the permission of the Portuguese King. The first Theatine sent for propagation to work in India landed in Goa in October, 1840[2].

In 1640, one of the Theatines priest Fr. Manco went to Bijapur, to work in the Golkonda Territory. From there he went over the Machilipatnam which was a port. Later he went over to Bhimilipatnam and built a Church. Ninteen members were baptised in that place Fr. Manco died at Bhimilipatnam in 1848[3].

Between 1640 and 1649 a total of 43 Theatine missionaries left Europe for India. The most notable to work in Andhra were Manaldini. Burgmore and Galco. After a break of some years, they continued the work which had been started by Fr Manco at Machilipatnam and Bhimilipatnam. Some more churches were built at places like Panapally, Corange and Narasapur. But it does not seen that the Theatines had any success in evangelizing the people of Andhra[4]. When Fr. Bargamora died in 1693, these churches were handed over to the Augustinians by the administrators of the diocess of Mylapur[5].

During the same years, a few Augustinians were working in some places of Andhra. In 1652 a church was established Bhanagar (Bhagyanagar) near the Court of the Sultan of Golkonda. It had 100 Christians, most of them were Portuguese. Six miles away from Bhanagar, a third church was erected in 1652, which had 300 Christians. The Augustinian churches were taken over by the Theatines at, Narasapur, Visakhapatnam, Corange, Bhminipatnam and Srikakulam. All these places altogether had a Christian population of about 400. All these Christians were travellers from elsewhere or their dependents and their slaves. The Augustinians also did not succeed in evangelizing any large group of people in Andhra, hence it cannot be said that Christianity was established in Andhra upto 17th century[6].

The French Jesuits of Pondicherry made their first efforts in Chittoor District in the first decade of the 18th century and from there the work spread to Ananthapur District and to the territory of the Raja of Venkatagiri, in the Nellore District. Within thirty years 16 stations were established and some thousands of caste converts gathered[7].

The war of the Austrian succession, in which the French and English took opposite sides, spread to India. Even after the treaty of Aix-la-chapelle in 1748, the war continued there through the intrigues of the French to gain control over the Nawab of the Carnatic and the Nizam of Hyderabad[8]. This forced many people to move north-east to the Northern circars, where they could live under the protection of the French. This areas was given to the French in 1753 in return for the services of the Marquis de Bussy to the Nizam in training his army. They settled on lands given to them in Nellore and Guntur Districts. But in 1785, the English took over the Northern Circars. With the defeat of the French troops, the area came under British control, whereupon followed the later suspension of the Jesuit order in 1773[9].

The first Protestant missionary to visit the Andhra desa was, Bartholomew Zieganbalg, who was also the first Protestant Missionary to India. On one of his visits to Madras he stopped at Tirupati at the temple and did some preaching there, but he was resisted by the local people[10]. Later his successor, Benjamin Schultz, started his work among the Telugus shortly after his arrival to Madras in 1728[11].

His successor John Philip Fabricius also continued to work among the Telugu people in Madras, but when the French occupied Fort St. George in 1748, the mission building was destroyed and Fabricus moved to Pulicat. Hence no efforts were made to extent Christianity among the Telugu until the rise of modern missions[12].

The era of Baptists began in India after the dedicated work of the Serampore missionaries, in the early decades of 19th century. They were interested to start a Telugu Mission called Baptists of England, but it was abandoned[13]. By the middle of the 19th Century the American Baptist Mission started its work in Andhra.

Rev. Samuel Day and Rev. E.L. Abbot arrived in Calcutta in 1836[14]. Day was the founder of the American Baptist mission among the Telugus in India[15]. From Srikakulam, he began to tour the surrounding villages[18]. Although a favourable beginning had been made. Mr. Day did not feel satisfied that it was the place for the permanent mission. In consultation with Mr. Malcom it was decided to move the mission to Madras to which city he and Mrs. Day proceeded, arriving there on March 17th, 1837 exactly one year from the date of his arrival at Vizagapatnam[17]. In 1837 he organised extensive tours between Vizagpatnam and Madras. Mr. Day moved from Madras to Nellor in 1840, which was the permanent settlement mission station for the Telugu missions of the American Baptists[18].

In early 1874 a Canadian Baptist missionary society established its first station in Telugu country at Coconada (Kakinada) and slowly spread its preaching to Tuni, Gunnapudi. Akividu and along the Krishna River[19]. In the Telugu Baptist Church Kurnool, a new station was opened in 1875 by Rev. D.H. Drake, Rev. W.G. Boggs opened a Church at Cumbbam. In the following year Narasaraopet, Bapatla and Vinukonda stations were opened. Then Kanigiri become a separate station in 1892. Podili, Donakonda and Sathenaspalli in 1894 and Gurzalla in 1885. Then the Baptist missions were started in the Nizams state. The Hunumakonda mission station was established in 1879 with five workers from Nellore. In 1895 in Nalgonda and in 1900 in Suryapet and Janagam mission stations were opened[20].

The London Missionary society, established its first contact in Vizagpatnam in 1805, and thus became the first Protestand Mission to start its work in Telugu country[21]. The pioneering Missionaries were George Gram, Des Grauges and Garden and Pritchett were their successors. These Missionaries and Gorden and Pritchett who followed them, were leaders in the translation of the Telugu scriptures and made a real contribution to the field of Telugu Christian Literature. At the same time they developed good schools and preached regularly to the local people, yet the Mission had to wait thirty years for its first convert Purushothama Chowdary[22].

The London Missionary society opened its second centre in the Rayalaseema districts, Cuddapah, Bellary, Ananthapur and Kurnool[23]. These ceded districts were given over to British by the Nizam of Hyderabad in 1880[24]. Rev. Howell Williams was sent in November, 1822 to establish a Mission station. The work was based at Cuddapah and the mission here was much more successful than the one in Visakhapatnam[25].

In 1824 they built a church building which was said to be the first Christian church building in Andhra[26]. Howell toured around Pulivendala Taluk and was able to convert ten pupils to Christianity. After Hawell left the country, London Missionary Society (hereafter called as L.M.S.) sent another missionary to preach in Nandyala, Jammala Madugu, Gothi, Kalapuram Taluks and opened

Christian centres at these places. In Kurnool district very few Madigas become Christians as a result of the work of the society for the propagation of the Gospel and the L.M.S. It was only after John E. Clough, Baptist Missionary from Ongole along with Rev. D.T. Drake toured Kurnool District as far as Kurnool in November, 1875, that converts from Madigas were made in numbers[27].

Mr. John Goldingham, the Collector of Machilipatnam District, the founder of Church Missionary Society invited Mr. Noble to Machilipatnam. The missionary work began in 1841, with R.T. Noble and H. Fox in Machilipatnam. After the arrival of Noble, the Evangelical and Educational work started[28].

They went from place to place preaching and visited Kankipudu, Bontupudi, Mylavaram, Rajahmundry, Samalkot, Kakinada, Bhadrachalam and Dummugudem. Their efforts, however, gained only three converts[29]. The first converts from Noble's school were two in 1847, followed by two more in 1852 and three more in 1855[30]. Two other towns Ellore and Vijayawada saw the establishment of centres by the Church Missionary Society in 1854. It was followed by Raghavapuram in 1870, Amalapuram in 1878 and Khammamett in 1888[31].

The next Protestant Mission was started by Mr. Bowden and Mr. Beer, the Plymouth Brethern Missionaries who came to India under the leadership of Anthony N. Groves[32]. They established the mission station at Narsapur in the Godavari District. The mission was called the Godavari Delta Mission, as it was established in the delta of the Godavari River[33].

The Wesleyan Methodist Church was first encouraged by Sir Arthur Cotton who was an Engineer of the Madras Government working on the Godavari River[34].

In December, 1878, special services were held for the soldiers in Secunderabad and a Methodist class was formed. The first Methodist Telugu service was held at Ramkoti in Hyderabad city in December, 1879 in the house of Mr. Joseph Cornelius, a Telugu Christian who had migrated from Madras to work in the villages[35].

The Lutherans are the most prominent of the missionaries in the Delta areas They early history of the Evangelical Lutheran Mission started with John Christian Fedrick Heyer. As Heyer himself recorded, January 4th, 1843 was the actual beginning of the American Lutheran Mission in Guntur[38]. Rev. Heyer commenced his work immediately with the help of an interpreter. By the middle of October, 1842, Father Heyer established schools in Prathipadu, Nallapadu and Kothapeta. In November he organised the first Hindu school in Guntur with an enrollment of fifteen pupils. This school was supported by Mrs. Walker, the wife of Justice Walker[37]. In two years he collected a small congregation of Native Christians.

On March 8th, 1844, Father Heyer with Vallet, a Northern German Missionary, started a tour to Palnad. They travelled through Phirangipuram, Narasaravupet, Piduguralla, Dachapalle, Pondugal and Gurzala. They continued their tour to Durgi. Karampudy and Bellamconda[38]. The tour was not fruitful. On January 15th, 1884 Heyer baptized three persons. Isaac and Ruth and their son Prakasam, a total of six since the beginning[39].

On 18th June, 1884, Mr. & Mrs. Gunn arrived at Guntur. On September, 1848 there were 32 converts in Guntur[40]. At the beginning of 1849, Father Heyer made a little progress among the Hindus. He had been active in working among the European residents of Guntur[41].

Heyer started his second tour to Palnad accompanied by the Rev. Beer of the Plymouth Brethern Mission, Narasapur, and Rev. F.A. Heise of Rajahmundry[42]. But the only Protestant Indian Christian in Palnad before Father Heyer's tour of 1849 was Maraputla John, whom Mr. Gunn had baptized in Guntur in 1847[43]. Heyer toured Chintapally, Gurzala and Pollepally, and he baptized 22 persons[44]. In Poliepally Heyer converted people from seven different families, and they came from three different village Pollepalli, Raghavapuram and Veldurthi. The converts belonged to weaver and Mala castes. Then he proceeded to Adigoppuls and Karempudi, arriving at Narasapur. Missionaries Gunn and Groenning joined

Heyer at Guruvayapalem near Narasaravupet. They attended the Kotapakonda festival, and then went on to Vinukonda, Martutur and Chilakalurpet and then arrived to Guntur. In Palnad Heyer baptized 34 peaople[45]. Thus Gurzala became the second station of merican Lutheran Mission in 1849. ☐Heyer started his proselyti ation starting schools and extensive tours around Guntur. The e was a strong opposition from the native Hindus especially from rahmins, for instance upon the mission work in Madras. Heyer wro e in the **Lutheran Observer** "The native congregations are small and a bitter spirit of opposition to the gospel is manifested by the Hathen inhabitants of Madras. The missionaries some times fin it necessary to call upon the police for protection, more esp cially during their evening appointments. When the Natives some t mes collect in large numbers, throw stones and show a disposit on to exercise mob law. The government otherwise maintains a cer ain neutrality in religious matters"[46]. ☐In Guntur Father Heyer, in ended to build a mission house in the centre of the Guntur bazz r, but there was so much obhectioin on the part of the Brahm ns that was opposition even for the starting of a school in G razal for low caste converts especially out castes as

within the Hindu caste system out caste people are prohibited to Iearn. When Heyer petitioned the court, the Native Judge gave a legal security for the school. In retaliation to this court order, a dispute on access to water arose in the Adagopala village between Malas and high castes. The high castes attacked an out caste for using water from their reservoir. Once again Heyer intervened. On the petition from Heyer, A Purvis the Guntur circar acting Collector directed the Magistrate to look after the dispute. The judgement was favourable to the weavers and established out castes "right to get water"[47]. As the work was thus progressing Rev.G.J. Martz, arrived at Guntur in 1850. Rev. Heyer left the field in 1852[48].

Rev. L.M. Vallet started the Northern German Missionary work in India in 1845 at Rajahmundry[50]. In 1855 the Revs. C.W. Groenning and A. Heise were sent out to assist him. Ellore and Rajahmundry were the primary mission fields, with Anglo-vernacular schools established at both the plaes. A number of elementary schools were opened in neighbouring villages. In 1851, as a consequence of financial constraints in Germany, the Northern mission society was obliged to with draw from their Indian field, and transferred the mission to the American Lutheran mission Society. Mr. Valet joined London missionary Society and started a mission at Chicacole. Mr. Heise remained incharge of the Rajahmundry station and Mr. Groeming had to give up Ellore and proceed to Guntur. For about eighteen years the Guntur and Rajahmundry mission had been connected with and managed by the American Lutheran Mission Society[51].

In 1856 the mission in Guntur. Palnad and Rajahmundry was under the charge of Mr. Groenning. Mr. Heige came in 1857, and in 1858 Mr. Unangst to Guntur and Mr. Long to Rajahmundry. He opened a new mission school at Samalkottah in 1859. In 1862 Mr. Heise retired and Mr. Groenning came back to Rajahmundry[52].

With the recommendation of Mr. Groenning, Mylius reached Rajahmundry in 1865. He made Naidupet his head quarters. This Hermannsberg mission established nine stations in this district between Madras and Nellore[53]. In 1869, due to the absence of the Lutheran missionaries in Rajahmundry, the Church mission Society took charge of Rajahmundry. In 1870 there were two different Boards, one of the General Synod supporting the Guntur and Palnad missions, the other of the General Council incharge of the Rajahmundry and Samalkot Station[54].

Rev. L.L. Uhl arrived in Guntur in March 1873. There after a series of missionaries came to India. In 1881, Kate Boggs arrived in Guntur. Dr. Wolf, Dr. Kugler and Miss Dryden in 1863, Dr. Durger and Dr. Macauley, Rev. Backer in 1898 and in 1900. Dr. E. Neudoerffer and Rev. G. Mathews arrived at Guntur[55]. The Rajahmundry and Guntur fields which were under two different organisations were now united as the Lutheran Church. The Andhra Evangelical Lutheran Church was organised in 1927[56].

Wesley started Episcopal Methodist Society in 1850 in America. J.H. Gordon, a CMS missionary, landed in Ballary in 1886 and travelled all the nearby villages like Tandore, Singanapally, Gannavaram. In 1905 another missionary C.E. Parker came to Hyderabad. He established an school in 1906 at Kakinada, another in 1910 at Jahirabad[57]. Salvation Army Society was established in 1865 in London by Sir William Booths an Methodist. Formerly it was called as East London Mission. In Telugu area they have branches in Ellore, Tanuku, Tenali, Nidubrolu, Bapatla, Gudiwada, Rajahmundry, Madras and Hyderabad[58].

In Ellore they established two high schools which are still working and one college in Hyderabad. The main office was situated in Madras. This society also ran medical dispensaries in ellore and Nidubrolu. At Bapatla, a Leper Hospital was established[59]. The full title of the Society which carried on the Dornakal mission is the Indian Society of Tinnevally. This indigenous mission was established in 1903 in Pallakottam in the Tinnevally district[60]. They established their first station in Warangal. They established a girls. High school and in 1907 they spread to Manukota, Singaral, Pakala areas. In 1906 there were twenty three converts. It was merged in Church of South India in 1922[61].

The Mulugu mission was separated from the Tirunavalli mission in 1917. Mulugu was taluk in Warangal district. Kanikella Sundaram, founder of the mission, converted a number of sudras[62]. In 1924 some converts from the Church of South India started the Allampur mission. Allampur is a taluk in Mahaboobnagar district[63].

In the same way the Church missionary Society has established the Parakala mission in 1927. Parakala was a taluk in the Warangal district[64]. There were a number of new societies which started their proselytising work in the successive decade like the India mission in 1930 in Charyala, Jangagham taluk, Indian Penthecoast Gospel Society at Ellore in 1932, Araku valley mission near Vishakaptanam in 1934, and Bible mission in 1938 at Rajahmundry[65].

The early successor of the missions established in the Telugu Speaking area was achieved with the support of the East India Company officials and the English residents in the mission centres[66]. After the 1813 Act, there is a shift in British Government policy not only in accepting missionaries in India but also giving guaranteed protection to christians in the exercise of their faith as to those of other religions. It shows that the East India Company became more conscious of the long term benefits of such support and activity[67].

In the same way East India Company officials for instance Mr. Goldingham, the Collector of Machilipatnam, was personally interested in the evangelisation of India. He first applied to the S.P.G. which found itself unable to undertake a fresh field, then to the C.M.S. When the Church Missionary Society refused his request on the ground of lack of funds, he personally offered to give or guarantee the necessary money. Even then the CMS was unable to find suitable men. Then Goldinggham himself personally invited two C.M.S. missionaries Mr. Noble and Fox in 1841[68]. hen he moved to Guntur, he established a school and worked for the ope ing and extension of christian work.   Mr. Henry Stokes follow d him in Guntur and was there when Father Heyer reached Gunt r. Concerning the Guntur field and the Collector of Guntur, Father Heyer wrote, "We went on our way from village to village until w reached Guntur, on July 31, 1842. Here we met with a very kind reception from H. Stokes, an ardent friend of missions and miss onaries as a very exemplary christian gentlemen. The inducements which Mr. Stokes held out and the kind offers of assistance w ich he made were far preferable to anything th

I could expect at Ongole, hence I decided in favour of Gu tur and after prayerful consideration concluded to commence mi sionary operation in Guntur forthwith"[69]. Stokes personality took initiative to request various American missionary societies. He wrote to them "That you will try to send us more missionaries...

unless you do, I fear our devoted labourers will sink under their burdens"[70]. Even after Stokes left for England in 1858, he continued to show keen interest in the Guntur mission, especially the Palnad mission field. He relieved it of all financial indebtedness to him and was frequently in correspondence with the Executive Committee of the Foreign Missionary Society, when they sought his advise[71].

In the same way Colonel Arthur T.Cotton, the engineering genius who played such a large part in the building of the great irrigation system in Rajahmundry, went out of his way to bring missionaries to the Godavari area with the assurance of moral and financial support from him. Cotton helped vallet to settle in Rajahmundry and Bowden of the Godavari mission was invited by Cotton to Dowleswaram to evangelical around the great labour camps brought there by the colonial rulers to build the Anicut across the Godavari river[72]. One of the ablest assistants to Colonel cotton was Lieutenant, later Major General, Felix Thackerey Hair, who proved to be a greater friend to Christian mission. Cotton and Hair invited CMS to establish mission in the Telugu area. CMS established their mission with help of the officers. Assistant collector, Hennry Newill of Guntur and Narasaravupet not only contributed for school but also helped missionaries in influencing the native Rajas and obtaining of properties[73]. These are the most notworthy officials to help the spread of thre missionary activities in Andhra.

The changed attitude of the Company and the general perception that the missionaries would serve the Long tern interests of the Empire, created a conductive atmosphere and situation in which they could expand their activities.

REFERENCES

1.   Census of India, 1891, Vol : XIII, Madras, 1893, P.63 also, Tekkedath Joseph : History of Christianity in India Vol. II, Bangalore, PP.298

2.   Tekkedth Joseph : History of Christianity of India Op. Cit., P.298.

3.   Ibid., p.299

4.   Ibid., p.301

5.   Ibid., p.302

6.   Ibid., p.306

7.   M.L. Dolbeen, A History of Lutheranism in Andhra Desa, 1842-1920, New York, 1959, p.35, also census of India 1891, Op.cit.p.63

8.   Dolbeer, Lutheranism in Andhra Op.cit.p.235

9.   Dolbeer, Lutheranism in Andhra, Op.cit., 0.35

10. Broomley, They were men sent from God, 1937, p.16. also Life and Letters of John Christian Fedrick Heyer M.D. Gospel Witness, May - 1940, p.349.

11. Dolbeer : Lutheranism in Andhra - Op.cit., p.36

12.   Ibid. : Trueman, B.H. Suez: A study of the Ongole mass movement and its impact on converts Madigas, United Theological College, Bangalore, 1984, p.27 (An unpublished, Bacholar of Divine thesis)

13.   Ibid., p.27

14.   Dolbeer, Op.cit., 37-38

15.   Drack and Kuder, The Telugu mission of the Evangelical Lutheran Church in North America, Philadelphia, 1914, p.46, also, Ritcher Julius : A History of Missions in India, London, p.153.

16.   David Dowmie. The Love Star, Philadelphia, p.24

17.   Ibid : 26-27

18.   Rev.R. Methew : A short history of one hundred years of the American Baptist mission 1836-1936, p.78.

19.   Drach & Kunder : The Telugu mission, Op.cit., p.170 also, W.G. Carder, on the beginnings of the Canadian Foreign mission to India, Indian Church History review, June 1969, p.135-143.

20.   W.G. Carder, Op.cit.135-143; Rev R. Mathew, A short history of A.B.M. p.78-90. Information extracted about Baptist missions from.

M.A. Sherring, Protestant missions in India, (from their commence in 1706 to 1871) London, 1875, pp.406-409

G. Herbert Ware, Christian missions in Telugu country, pp.201-205.

21. Drach and Kunder, The Telugu Mission, Op.cit., p.458, sherring, A History of protestant mission - Op.cit., p.458.

22. Dolbeer, Lutheranism in Andhra, Op.cit., pp.37-38.

23. Drach and Kunder, Op.cit., p.46

24. Ibid., Ritcher, A History of Protestant missions, Op.cit., 0.153

25. David Downie. The Lone Star, Op.cit., p.240

26. Herbertware, Christian Missions, Op.cit., pp.201-204

27. Ibid.

28. Herbertware, Christian Missions, Op.Cit., P.201-204.

29. Ibid., June 1927, P.45

30. Ibid., 192

31. The above material also, extracted from : C.H. Swavely, Life and Letters of J.C.F. Heyer, Missionary to India, Gospel Witness, May 1940, P.357.

32. T. Devadas, The Caste in the Church in Andhra, Rajahmundry, Andhra - Theological College, 1977, P.28 (unpublished thesis for Bachelor of Divine).

33. Ibid., P.28

34. Ibid., P.26

35. Ibid., P.27

36. Ibid., P.29

37. Rev. C.H. Swavely, Missions to India, 1841-45; Gospel Witness, May 1940, P.359.

38. Ibid., P.36. Quoted from Father Heyers own story, P.65-75.

39. Ibid., P.361

40. Ibid., P.362

41. Lutheran Observer, May 24, 1848, P.159

42. Swavely, The first Furlogh 1840-47, Returned to Guntur, 1848, Gospel Witness, 1940, P.385.

43. Ibid., Quoted from Lutheran Observer, July 27, 1849, P.119.

44. Ibid., Quoted from Lutheran Observer, June 18, 1847, P.188, and December 31, 1847, P.71.

45.   Life and Letters of Father Heyer, H.D. Swavely, Protestant Missions in the Palnad 1849-1952. Gospel Witness, July, 1940, p.412.

46.   Ibid., P.413, for other details about Palnad Mission "The Missionary, 1849, P.187. Swavely, Missions to India, 1841-45, Gospel Witness, May, P.381.

47.   Life & Letters of Father J.F.C. Heyer, Swavely, The first Furlongh, 1846-47; Return to Guntur 1848, Gospel Witness, P.384.

48.   Father Heyers own stay, Lutheran observer, August 19, 1851, P.583, cited in Gospel Witness, Feb., 1943, P.243.

49.   Rev. E. Unangst, American Lutheran Mission (General Synod), Indian Missionary Conference 1879, also Rev. H.C. Schmidt American Evangelical Lutheran Mission (General Council) Indian Missionary Council, cited in Gospel Witness, July 1942, P.389-409.

50.   Swevely (ed.) One hundred years in the Andhra Country, Madras, 1942, P.343-57.

51.   Ibid.

52.   G. Krupachari, Telugu Sahityaniki Krastavulaseva, Hyderabad, P.49

53.   Ibid., 49-50.

54.   Ibid., P.50.

55.   Herbertware, Christian Missions, Op.Cit., P.205.

56.   Krupachari, Telugusahityaniki, Op.Cit., P.54.

57.   Ibid.

58.   Ibid., P.55

59.   Ibid.

60.   Ibid., P.50-56

61.   M.L. Doolbeer, The History of Lutheranism, Op.cit., P.87

62.   Ibid., P.88

64.   Bobwilliams, Research studies in the economic and social environment of the Indian Church (undertaken in preparation for the meeting of the International Missionary Council at Tamburam - December, 1938, P.8-9, and the Dornakal Doicesan Magazine, June, 1927, P.45.

65.   Life and Letters of J.C.F. Heyer, M.D., Swavely, The First Furlongh, 1846-47, return to Guntur, 1849, Gospel Witness, June, 1940, P.384, also : Lutheran Observer, July 26, 1850, P.324, Indian Missionary Conference, 1879, cited in Gospel Witness, July 1942, P.391.

66.   Lutheranism in andhra, Op.cit., P.90

67.   Ibid.,

68.   Ibid.,

69.   The Missionary, February, Feb, 1849, P.79, cited in Gospel
       Witness, 1940, P.381.

70.   Ibid.,

71.   Ibid.,

72.   Ibid.,

73.   Dolbeer, Lutheranism in Andhra, Op.cit., P.90-91.

CHAPTER-3
THE QUESTION OF CASTE

One of the major social issues that the Missionaries had to deal with was the question of Caste, an unique aspect of Indiansocial order. Caste was an important factor influencing conversion and creating distinctions within the Indian Christian community. This chapter examines several different aspects of this issue. Why did the early missionaries allow caste distinctions in the Church, especially the Roam Catholic and also within the Lutheran denominations. With the available material we may analyse the political and social conditions of the early days of Christianity. The missionaries who came to India to preach the Gospel, they did not launch a direct attack against caste because knowledge of the historical background of the institutions was partial and because of the missionary's desire to spread the Gospel without offending the British East India Company. The latter had strict rules prohibiting the missionary from getting involved in anything that would disturb the established order and create unrest.

Secondly why the sudden consciousness about the caste distinctions in the Church, what immediate measures and methods did they utilise what impact did anti-caste resolution have on the christian community.

Finally the missionary methods through the British government, acts and resolutions among christian conferences to eradicate caste distinctions among the christian church are studied.

In Indian social order the Caste system played an out standing part. It was at once the product of Hinduism. Census of India defined it "Caste has been defined as an endogamous group or collection of such groups bearing a common name and having some traditional occupation the members of which are so linked together by these and other ties, such as the tradition of common origin and the possession of the same tutelary deity and the same social status ceremonial observance and the firmly priests, that they regard themselves, and are regarded by the others, as forming a single homogeneous community"[1].

J. Pickett's opinion was "a Caste is an exclusive endogamous, hereditary cooperative group, bound together by the tradition of a common origin and a body of common custom"[2]. When discussing the economic aspects of caste some missionaries declared that originally caste had some economic advantage because of the fact that occupations were hereditary, the knowledge and skill acquired by the father descends to the son. In this way the Indian crafts had reached certain levels of perfection. But the essence of caste was not to admit of change because of this technical and industrial arts of Europe soon outstripped those of India. By making occupations hereditary by caste, this may have encouraged development upto a point, but it wasted the talent of those who were more suited to employment in something more than hereditary occupations and successfully prevented the infusion of new ideas[3]. J.N. Farquhar declared that old caste restrictions prevented the development of lower caste by the tyranny of caste[4].

Talking about Caste in the early churches Roman Catholics never attacked the caste system directly. They recognize Caste in its social aspect as an inevitable feature of Indian life and therefore allowed for a caste wise stratification which tolerated untouchability. It was hoped that a gradual growth in Roman catholic church for instance-would bring about some change[5].

St. Francis Xavier on the kerala fishery coast allowed different Churches. In the 17th century Fr. De-Nobili allowed in the same building different places with a low wall of separation Even the Lutheran mission of earlier time regarded Caste as a social phenomenon and with few exceptions tolerated Caste division among their converts[6]. Caste based distinctions with in the early Catholic congregations did not come under very serious attack until the 19th century when the Anglicans entered in the Indian missionary scene[7].

In the North Indian Churches Caste was apparent among the converts. In the Bengal and Bombay presidencies the missionaries had insisted on its exclusion from the churches form the very beginning8. However in South India, where the Caste feelings in general were stronger than in the North[9], the Protestant missionaries had allowed some Caste practices within the Church[10]. Caste had become strongly entrenched especially in some areas for example the Society for Propagation of the Gospel (SPG), Anglican missions originally conducted by the Danes. A survey conducted in the Tanjore mission in 1828 revealed, for example, that at church the Christians of high Caste still sat on the right side of the pulpit, and also the high Caste christians still refused to intermarry or eat with the lower Caste converts[11].

The Caste system was very prominent among Kerala Christians. For instance high caste converts though within the social sphere they were absorbed as the Syrian christians, there was a lot of distinctions among higher and lower Caste converts. Castes like Ezhavas and palayas and Harijans even after conversion they were treated as untouchable in the church. The old christians were called as Syrian Christians and the Harijan Christians were called as Puttu Christians (New-Christians), the Charmar Christians, Pulaya Christians etc. The Syrian Christians were considered Superior to all others. This discrimination is reflected in the organisation of the catholic church. A similar phenomenon is seen in Andhra as well. The new caste problems and tensions were brought into the churches such as those between converts from the main and Madiga castes in Telugu country[13].

In the catholic churches in Kalvanoor there were many converts from the lower Castes. Untouchables make up 83 percent of the catholic christian population in Kalvanoor parish. We find the effects of caste with in the Church, the untouchable and Malainam, udayam christians sat in different place in the church[13]. This development can be traced from the 17th century when Fr. De Nobili allowed different caste in the same building in different places with a low wall of separation14.It was with arrival of the new Anglican missionaries early in the 19th century that sensitive question was brought to a climax when they witnessed number of high caste converts refusing to sit with low caste converts and refusing to have any social dealings with them[15].

Between 1807 and 1827 there was a vigorous Move among the new missionaries and they induced the authorities to oppose all the caste distinctions among the Indian Christians16. The attitude towards caste was similar to that of all protestant missions especially most, of the Telugu Lutheran Groups led a continued struggle caste.

It was evident that the Lutheran missions considered caste as opposed to the very core of the christian faith and not merely a social custom of the people[18]. Mylius felt it was a great evil and that he would be disobedient to god and betray the Indian people if he were lenient in the matter[19]. In the Telugu speaking area of Guntur the Lurheran mission had converts primarily from the out caste and thus the problem did not stand out as much as elsewhere in kerala, for example[20].

Rev. J. Henriohs, American Baptist missionary in describing the caste structure in the Telugu country, referred to the non-caste people, the Madigas, who were a fourth of the population. "These are farm labourers or serfs, they live by day labourer cooly work. They are also artisans and so called caste occupations of the Madigas is Leather dressing and show making while the malas engaged in weaving"[21].

Heyer writing in an earlier period, pionted out the likely historical context with in the which the malas as a distinct caste group came into existence. Heyer wrote "A very numerous class of the poor in India are called Mala people, most of the weavers belong to this class. It is pretty certain that these malas descended from original inhabitants of the land, who have been conquered by the other invading tribes, were reduced to a state of servitude. When the Brahmanical religion was introduced into India these Malas were considered as out castes and the some respects were treated worse than slaves"22.

The protestant missions especially in Guntur region the majority of converts are from the so-called out castes. Malas and Madigas, like kerala churches where the difference between the low caste and high caste converts was present, the same phenomena become very prominent among the Telugu christians particularly in Guntur surrounding areas. in Guntur Luthern mission, Heyer points out, the males and madigas among converts the mala people belong neither to the Brahmanical nor sudra caste, but are considered as out castes from among the higher classes. The males are almost as tenacious of their ranks as the Brahmans of their, and as fear full to losing it'23 Heyer revealed his own experience with this problem 'I engaged a man of lower rank than malas to do work in the kitchen. They have given a great offense to the males in those village especially where a number has professedly embraced christianity"24

Father Heyer reveals the growth of caste feeling among the converts in Guntur especially in Luthern mission. "A mala convert used to take the communion wine out of one and the same cup with the madiga convert. It was but a few years ago when this was sternly objected to and number of Mala converts refused to commune at the same table with the Madiga converts"[25]. This change in the attitude of Mala converts refused to commune at the same table with the Madiga converts[25]. In Guntur the Lutherans were very strong, their largest in gatherings were from among the Malas, though thousands of Madigas also entered the Lutheran fold. Nevertheless more madigas have become Baptists[27].

Caste distinctions became very severe in the Baptist and the Church of India congregations of Kurnool. A group of Malas converted into a Baptist congregation so the Madigas decided to join the other congregation, they were hesitant to join church of India, even though it accommodated both Mala and Madigas[28].

These distinctions were continued even in Tallapudi, in Rajahmundry surroundings and tensions between Malas and Madigas in different missions spread to other mission fields. Mr. Mc. Cready Missionary of Tallapudi explains "when Christianity first enteres a place should those who first embrace it to be of the Mala caste, which is one of the lower castes, others still lower will join us, but should the first converts to be chucklers or Madigas, the Malas keep aloof"[29].

There were many difficulties encountered in the schools started by the missions when the children of lower castes were enrolled. Father Heyer tells of his experience in one village in the Palnad area where the weavers refused to send their children to the newly established school because the teacher was of a lower caste[30]. The missionaries found some difficulties when they came to receive members into the church. At the time of Baptism the Schleswing-Holstain mission at Salur, fifteen of the members fell away almost as a body because of caste difficulties. For instance David a Catechist was a mala from Nellore, who had served the Harmannsburg mission. Two of the young boys, Nathaniel and Jeshua, refused to live with him as boarding pupils because of caste differences[31].

Bishop Wilson of the Church of England, in Calcutta, declared that the Christians shall not be separated according to caste. All the Protestant Missions attitude towards caste was similar to that of all Protestant Missions except the Leipzig Lutherans, who had inherited the lenient position of the old Tranqubar mission in Tamil Nadu[32].

Jean Dahl, Hermansberg missionary in Venkatagiri, associated with high caste people in his area, he was also a close friend of Raya Venkatagiri, converted a lot of high caste people. He came to the conclusion that he could accomlish more by adopting the lenient position of Liepzig mission. He believed that the converts, with their caste distinctions, would gradually change with the spirit of the God's word, rather than by strict church discipline. But he was recalled to Germany for his refusal to use Church discipline against caste practice[33].

The Lutheran mission Considered caste as opposed to the very core of the Chrisitian faith and not merely a social Custom of the people34. Mylius, a Hermennsber missionary of Rajahmundry, felt that caste is a great evil and would Split the congregation if missionaries were lenient to caste. Missionaries often took disciplinary action against the people who insist on caste in the church. They even excommunicate the person under disciplinary action[35].

In the Bombay missionary of October 1832 the missionaries discussed about the fight against the caste and they complained that the government was not doing anything to abolish caste[36]. In 1883 David Wilsion 6th Bishop of Calcutta (1832-58) strongly felt that the retention of caste was wrong and issued in his famous circular letter to Anglican missionaries through his Diocese (which included the whole of India) in which he declared that the distinction of caste must be abandoned decidedly, immediately and finally[37].

After the Wilson declaration a few years afterwards in 1848, Bishop Spencer and 84 clergy and missionaries of his diocese published a resolution in which they expressed their extreme concern that the "Heathen institute of caste" should have found any place in the Christian church and declared that its retention was incompatible with the spirit of the Gospel[38].

As Ingham has shown, individual missionaries like Rhenius and Rev.Mead of the Lutheran mission society grappled boldly with the problem and attempted to suppress caste practices among their converts, these efforts remained scattered and uncoordinated, these missionaries believed retention of caste with in the chruch was harmful to Christianity[39].

In 1878 Bishop Wilson's decision became a resolution in the missionary conference of South India and Ceylon that with reference to caste "It is the duty of all missionaries believed[41] that the caste among the Christians Which Was primarily a religious institution was based upto the concepts derived from Hinduism[42]. They argued that the caste distinctions as found among Hindus and that in both cases, caste was based on the idea of "Purity or impurity by birth." These qualities were conceived of Christians but by the Hindu religion, thus in retaining caste, convers retained an important part of their former religion.Caste being "one of the evil of heathenism which has unwarily and most unfortunately been allowed to accompany the native convert in his passage to Christianity"[43]. The objection was that in caste "these is an implicit idea of spiritual hierarchy which contradicts the idea of equality implicit in Christians (regardless of origin) were equaly members of the mystical body of Christ"[44].

In 1850 missionaries of the Madras missionary conference declared that "candidates for Baptism should be required to declare that they renounce caste usages forever in principals and practice"[45]. For this a definite attitude towards caste was considered between all the Anglican missionaries of Leipzing society among the Tamils in Madras and Tanjore. Most of the Madras missionary societies also appealed for the co-operation between the mission to deal with caste and also pleaded with all Protestant missions to adopt a similar policy. The policy was signed by Presbyterians, Methodists, Baptists congregationalists and others which was endorsed by the Calcutta and Bomaby missionary conference. It was published together as the Anglican statement in 1848[46]. Opposition to the retention of caste among converts was expressed repeatedly in resolutions carried out at South India missionary conferences held in 1858, 1879 and 1900[47].

After the firm resolutions against caste, the missinaries found that this approach was extremely costly and some times ineffective. For example the firm and decisive measures some times weakened their influence over their congregations. The worst part of it was part of the congregation walking out, declaring its independence, joining some other mission or else slipping back to Hinduism[48]. For example S.P.G. missions, especially were greatly reduced in size as result of the missionaries refusal to tolerate caste observations. In a report represented in 1860, one observer confessed for example, that all the missions of the Tanjore circle were suffering in the same way. The high caste converts felt they were degrading into the status of sudras. This became a prominent issue[49]. The strong repressive measures against caste with the church and the firm stand taken by Bishop Wilson and others failed to achieve long term, permanent result because their successors were weakminded bishops, missionaries and Pastors who allowed caste feelings to creep back in the church. Some missionaries argued that this policy was a gross - mistake[50].

Hence by the end of the century, there were two main schools of thought on the caste problem among the missionaries. On the one hand, some missionaries argue that the firmness did have a statutory effect and that was better to have few real Christians rather than many nominal adherents. On the other hand, there were missionaries who felt that with gentle persuasion and the gradual dissemination of Christian ideas, caste within the churches would gradually disappear[51].

Missionaries also attempted to ignore the caste distinctions in their schools, hospitals and medical dispensaries, Missionaries also frequently appealed to the government it self to ignore the caste in all its activities. For example in 1858 they appealed that the Government "to discountenance this absurd and injurious system by all proper methods and especially to take steps to prevent its recognisation in all its Government documents as well as officers and courts"[52].

Though out this period the missionaries argued that caste with its terrible cruelty and pride" led to injustice and suffering especially among the lower caste[53]. Missionaries also claimed that the caste system was a form of "tyranny" which stifled individual freedom and initiative and consigned the bulk of the population to" hopeless slavery"[54]. Besides this, the caste was deeply injurious to the welfare of the country at large[55]. It was claimed that caste retarded economic development, created social evils, handicapped social reform and impeded the growth of a healthy patriotic spirit.

The Rev. Painter believed that caste was responsible for many of India's most serious social evils "limits intermarriages to small communities by forbidding marriage with any outsiders. And preventing fresh individuals from becoming members, thus the affect is necessarily in time the intermarriage of near relations. It brings about child marriage and polygamy. For since it is disgrace for a girl to remain unmarried, as well as contrary to religious, very early marriages and polygamy became practically a necessity"[57].

In 1880 the Rev. Sherring, claimed that because of caste distinction the Hindu had no faith in disinterested patriotism and could not combine together on a large scale in any matter of national importance[58]. But after the foundation of national congress it could no longer be held that the Hindus were unable to combin together on matters of national importance, Mordoch argued that these combination were in spite of rather than because of cas e distinction[59]. The missionaries not only theoretically argued for the removal of caste but also practically. For example n 1893 the Caste Suppression Society was formed at Tuticorn to ounter act the practices of the caste among missionaries and past rs, of using caste titles when addressing members of the con regation and of following communicants to approach the altar i order of caste[60]. British did not singly take an anti caste osition. In theory they developed the means of making the Christ an independent of caste related occupations through the development of its industrial land agricultural programs which were importan factors in reducing the incidents of caste problems among the Basiel mission Christians[61]. For example, Serampore brotherhood established a self supporting unit which could accommodate new arrivals of their community like Sarampore missionaries paper mills, printing works offered sustenance to some of the converts.

Missionaries were active in distributing the anticaste literature between 1848 and 1868. British, American and other Protestant missionaries published tracts and pamphlets on the subject of caste in at least nine different languages. In Tamil, a tract describing the "unchristian character and evil tendencies of caste" passed through six editions in about twenty years. Fifty thousand copies of a tract in Bengali on the same subject were issued by the Calcutta tract and book society between 1850 and 1870, while a treatise on caste in Telugu passed through ten editions in eleven years[62].

the missionaries brought caste disability removal act (Act XXI of 1850). This legislation gave the authority of caste councils, by giving converts to Christianity and other non-Hindu religion right to inherit their ancestral   property63.

The effect of the missionaries on the caste system is by no means easy to ascertain. However, there can be little doubt that agitation and argument against caste, together with spread of Christian Indians, at least stimulated or reinforced Hindu attempts at reform. It was well known, for example, that Keshab Chandra Sen, 64 a fierce critic of the caste system was himself strongly influenced by Christianity to give another example, in western India, jotiba phuley founder of the Satya shodak Samaj which aimed at challenging Brahmin supremacy, and emphasised the fatherhood of man was educated in mission school where he was deeply influenced by Christian teaching on equality[65].

Missionary agitations and attempts to improve the condition of the out caste, this was partly because many converts coming from the depressed classes. The missionary was among the first to draw the government attention to their plight and disabilities. In 1891 for example, the Madras missionary conference urged the government of Madras to appoint a commission to inquire into the condition of the Pariah population[66]. In their petition they urged that for all intents and purpose slavery continued among pariahs and that these people faced almost insuperable obstacles in obtaining secure house sites, land and even elementary education[67]. Missionary work among these and other outcaste greatly impressed some Hindu observers and fear of loosing large number of Hindu population to Christianity spread educated Hindus into increased reform activity[68].

Apart from their effect in stimulating Hindu movements for reform of the caste system, the missionaries were also more indirectly, undermining the effectiveness of caste sanctions and weakening the power of caste sanctions over individuals. As Ghurye has commented, the effect of new British legal system in undermining the authority of the caste councils, in weakening their ability to impose sanctions was constantly to remind the people that "civil law is higher than caste law". But the legal system, expanding its usage and obligation, was as a result of the constant pressure of missionary as well as other activities. Though their precise formulation of caste and, by using the law courts, they frequenty before law in operation. Missionaries brought various cases in persecution before the law courts and won their cases. In Madras and Travancore for example, the missionaries were particularly active in establishing, the right of sharmars, the pariahs and christian converts to the use of public roads and national highways[69]. In Travancore, after serious disturbances, they also succeeded in establishing the legal rights of Shannar women to change the traditional dress by covering the upper part of their body[70].

But perhaps even more important than these triumphs was the success of the missionary campaign against the caste feeling which forbade certain castes from making use of public wells. The water question was probably one of the most frequent causes of disputes between Hindus and Christians[71]. And it was particularly acute in the river parts of Andhra (Telugu speaking area), where converts, increasing in numbers and moving out beyond the mission compound, did not have easy access to and alternative source of supply other than those already used by caste by Hindu. A major dispute rose over the christians using reservoirs used by Hindus and right of the christians to dip their cups in the Krishna river in madras presidency, with the missionary petition, the Magistrate gave a judgment in favour of christian converts72.

The attitude of the missionary towards the caste with in the church had to some extent met with some Opposition by the middle of 19th century. In subsequent years, there was increasing disagreement over how to tackle the problem. The missionary remained opposed in principal to caste among converts though out the period they were also extremely critical of caste as an institution among Hindus and do not appear to have greatly modify their attitude as the years progress. Missionaries persisted in attempts to eliminate to eliminate the influence of the caste in their own and in government institutions and practices and continued to campaign against various caste disabilities.

Moreover, a longer and more mature experience of caste within the christian church did not in the least weaken the feeling. no major development occurred during the 19th century. Encouragimg the adoption of a more sympathetic attitude towards caste either with in or outside churches was becoming quite common. Out side the church for instance, caste persisted as one of the most serious obstacles for the spread of Christianity.

As a result of the growth of cities the introduction of the new methods of transport, spread of education, the new system of equality before law and other reforms the caste system was becoming more flexible. Attitudes towards caste, especially among the educated classes and the authority of caste councils was in some cases undermined and many caste observances were no longer performed with such regularity. The missionaries played a part in this process of social change. Their arguments and agitations against caste probably influenced. Hindu reformers stimulated a desire for change. They publicised the condition of the out caste and, though their examples stimulated Hindu attempts to improve the lot of the Pariahs. The missionaries also played a part in the precise formulation of laws effecting caste by resorting to the law courts and winning their cases. They helped to undermine the effectiveness of the caste councils and weaken the caste regulation such as those restricting the use of public highways and wells. To eradicate caste in christian community was a real problem.It was a delicate issue to tackle because the influence of the caste with in the converts who slipped into either Hinduism or another christian congregation whenever they encountered a specific problem with caste. This fluid situation if the converts are more than the contributions are high. So this was also a practical reason why missionaries did not insist on the removal of the caste.

There is very clear evidence available on the different approaches of the Protestants and Roman Catholics towards caste. The Catholics with their own internal hierarchical pattern for instance of the Laymen to Bishop, had little moral difficulty in allowing caste distinctions in their congregation. For the Lutherans, the problem was more serious. They believed in the brotherhood of the community, with no hierarchy, was precisely why the Lutherans fought against the caste system. While the missionaries played a part in making the system more flexible and enforcing some change, they were not successful as they Wished in destroying caste consciousness.

REFERENCES

1. **Census of India**, 1911, Vol.1, Part-1, Report, P.367.

2. J.W. Pickett, **Christian Mass Movements in India**, New Fork, 1983, P.30.

3. Duncun B Forester, **Caste and Christianity**, London, 1880, P.138.

4. Parquhar, **Crown of Hinduism**, P.184.

5. C.B. Firth, **An Introduction to Indian Church History**, P.220.

6. C.B. Firth, Op., Cit., P.157.

7. Frykenberg, **I.E.S.H.R.,** Vol.XVII, P.12.

8. **Minute of the Madras Missionary Conference and other Documents on the subject of Caste (1850)**, P.25,32.

9. Oddie, **Social Protest in India**, New Delhi, 1979, P.44.

10. J.J. Prett, **Out Side the City**, London, 1962, P.32. Also C.B. Firth, Op., Cit., P.157.

11. Oddie, Op., Cit., P.45

12. Forrester, Op., Cit., P.79.

13. Oddie, Op., Cit., P.27.

14. C.B. Firth, Op., Cit., P.220.

15. E.K. Pillay, The impart of Christian Mission on Caste in Indian Society, **Indian Historical Records**, Allahabad, 1973, P.103.

16. Oddie, Op., Cit., P.45

17. M.L. Doolbeer, **A History of Lutheranism in the Andhra Desa**, 1842-1920, New York, 1959, P.125.

18. Ibid., P.127.

19. G. Drach, **Kingdom Path Finders**, P.45.

20. Quoted from proceedings, **General Synod, 1879**, P.55, Cited in Dolbeer, P.129.

21. **Report of the 3rd Decennial Missionary Conference 1892-93**, Bombay, P.550-59.

22. Father Heyer's own story, **Lutheran Observer**, August, 1851, P.583, Cited in **Gospel Witness**, Feb., 1943, P.243.

23. Father Heyers own story, **Lutheran Observer**, December, 1851, P.607, Cited in **Gospel Witness**, March, 1943, P.311.

24. Ibid.

25. **Indian Missionary Conference,** 1879, Cited in **Gospel Witness**, July 1942, P.404.

26. W.J. Picket, Op., Cit., P.336.

27. J.H. Proctor, Scottish Missionaries in India, An enquiry in motivation, **South Asia**, Vol.XIII, 1990, P.43-61.

28. Picket, Op., Cit., P.326.

29. H.L. Dolbeer, **The History of Lutheranism in Andhra desa**, New York, 1959, P.184.

30. Ritcher, **A History of Missions in India**, new York, 1907, P.239.

31. Dolbeer, Op., Cit., P.130.

32. Ibid., Op., Cit., P.126.

33. Ibid, Op., Cit., 127

34. Ibid., Op., Cit., P.130

35. Ibid, P.175

36. J. Bateman, **The Life of Right Rev. Danial Wilson D.D.**, London, 1860, Vol.I, P.434-435, and also see, John C Webster, **The Christian Community Change in 19th Century**, Mac Millan, Meerat, 1976, P.

37. Parcival, **The Land of Vedas**, London, 1856, P.496-502. Also see, H.E. Gibbs, **The Anglcan Church in India (1600-1970)**, P.35.

38. **Minute of the Madras Missionary**, 1850, P.34-39.

39. Ingham, O.p, Cit., P.73.

40. Oddie, Op., Cit., P.53

41. Parcival, **The Land of Vedas**, London, 1858, P.496-502. Also H.E. Gibbs, **The Anglican Church in India** (1800-1970), P.57.

42. Parcival, Op., Cit... P.503-5; 507, Oddie, Op. Cit.

43. Oddie, Protestant Missions caste and social change India 1850-1914 (Article) **I.E.S.H.R.** 1969, P.264. Also Y.B. Abbasayulu, **A Study Schedule Caste Elite in A.P.** (An unpublished Ph.D. thesis) Osmania University, Hyderabad, 1977, P.7.

44. Sharrok, **South India Missions**, P.185-6; 192-3; also Parcival, Op. Cit., P.507.

45. Oddie, Op. Cit., Quoted from **Minutes of Madras Missionary Conference**, F.10.

46. Oddie, **Social Protest**, P.47.

47. Oddie, **Protestant Missions,** Op., Cit., P.263.

48. Sharrock, **South India Missions**, West Minister, 1910, P.181, 194-43.

49. Oddie, **Protestant Missions**, Op. Cit., P.270. Quoted from **Digest of SPG Records**, London, 1883, P.514.

50. **Indian Evangelical Review**, Vol.III, April, 1878, P.509.

51. Sharrock, Op. Cit., P.183.

52.	Ibid., P.183.

53.	Oddie, **Protestant Missins**, Op. Cit., P.274.

54.	Parcival, Op. Cit., P.507.

55.	Murdoch (Ed), **Papers on Indian Reform**, caste, P.37. Cited in Oddie, **Protestant Missions**, P.283.

56.	Oddie, **Protestant Missions**, Op. Cit., P.28.

57.	Oddie, **Protestant Missions**, Op. Cit., P.281. Quoted from East and West, Vol.IV, Oct, 1908, P.440.

58.	Ibid., P.282, Quoted from prospects of Hindu caste, **Indian Evangelical Review**, Vol.VII, Oct, 1880, P.174.

59.	Oddie, Op. Cit., P.50.

60.	Ritcher, Op. Cit., P.169, David, Op. Cit., P.173.

61.	Ingham, Op. Cit., P.27.

62.	Ibid., P.46.

63.	Ibid, P.49.

64.	See, for further details, speech on Jesus Christ, Europe and Asia, In Kesab Chendersen, **Lecturer in India**, Calcutta, 1954, P.1-36.

65.	D. Keer, **Mahatma Jotiro Phooley - Father of Our Social Revolution**, Bombay, 1964, P.13-15; 92, 125-7. Also A.

Seal, **The Emergence of Indian Nationalism, Competition and Collaboration in the later nineteenth century**.

66. **Report of the 3rd Decennial Conference**, who are backward classes - also Cencus Report, 1881. The pariahs in Tamil, Malas in Telugu Holia in canasese, Poliyar in Malayahan and Dhedain Marathi in they are every were the menial servants of the country, census - 1881.

67. **Report of the 3rd Decennail Missionary Conference** held at Bombay, 1991-93, Vol.11, P.544-8, 574-5.

68. Farquhar, **Crown of Hiduism**, P.173, A.R. Desai, **Social Background of Indian Nationalism**, Bombay, 1968, P.266-7.

69. G.S. Ghurey, **Caste Class and Occupation**, Bombay, 1961, P.180-82.

70. Mateer, **Native Life in Travancore**, London, 1833, P.335-338.

71. Hardgrave, The Breast-cloth controversy, The caste consciousness in South-Travancore, The **I.E.S.H.R.** Vol.V., No.2, June 1968, P.171-187, J. Mullens, **A Brief Review of Ten Years Missionary Labour in India**, London, 1963, P.106-7.

72. **Harvest Field**, Vol.IV, April, 1893, P.44-5.

CHAPTER-4
MISSIONS AT WORK

An important aspect of Missionary work was Conversion. In Andhra, Conversions underwent a gradual phase of change, individual and small group conversions of the early 19th century, were replaced at the end of the 19th century by mass conversion movements. This chapter discusses the process of the conversions. Conversion from Hindu religion to Christianity, changing into a totally different social and cultural religion and identity is an interesting subject to deal with conversions made in early days, were mostly from individual micro families and lower and upper castes. During the second half of the 19th century, the conversions become rapidly mass movements.

Another major question attempted to be answered is what were the methods utilized by the missionaries in conversion and its significance. Lastly, what has been the specific role of caste as one invisible part of mass conversion.

In a mass-movement or a group movement the converts tend to move simultaneously together with his family, relatives and other belonging to the same social group in to the fold of religion. That is to preserve at least the basis of his social environment. This can be analyzed as a group or village conversion, a major social decision rather than an individual one. Some time the group leaders faith make the whole group or village to convert to Christianity. The conversion of such a group does not mean that every member of it has a fully formed faith, it means that the group has been willing to accept Christian training and discipline.

Oddie defined conversion as "a process by which people move out of one religious community into another"[1]. C.B. Firth lists out the motives for a conversion as follows[2].

1. Spiritual motives

2. Secular motives (eg. financial support)

3. Social reasons (eg. improvement of social status)

4. Natal influence (eg. a child become a Christian because of his parents Conversion)

The early conversions took place among individuals who were economically independent and spread to the poor and more independent individuals or micro families converted from both lower and upper castes. According to C.B. Firth the earliest conversions were motivated by spiritual motives. These individual conversions involve more than a change of belied. It involved a transfer from one society to another, from the Hindu fold to the Christian church3.

For the early Baptist high caste converts, to leave one's caste was a more serious matter. The converted high caste people tended to become a denationalized person, cut off from his people and obliged to associate with Europeans and to live in small artificial Indian Christian communities consisting of individuals, out off from the Hindu religion. They were treated like outside caste and illtreated by friends and relatives[4]. Describing the situation in Machilipatnam in 1866 Rev.A.H.Arden pointed out "as the first converts have to be protected by police--it was very rare a high caste convert ever reestablished any kind of contact with their families, they were isolated by Hindu society[5]" those who wanted to convert into Christianity also had the fear of being illtreated by their friends and relatives so they had to completely depend upon the mission. All this made individual especially high caste conversion very rare.

It's a mistaken idea to assume that the outcaste had nothing to lose by becoming Christian. Although he had a little wordily goods, they could be ostracized by the community, refused an opportunity to work, and denied the use of water and washing privileges. His own people could react very harshly to any sign of independence from group loyalty. For a man and his family in the beginning of the Christian movement to dare to separate from his group and accept the Christianity was unthinkable[6].

Generally the missionaries were always willing and ready to fight for the rights of the converts. For example Rev.Earnest Neudoerffer in Rajahmundry field around Bhimavaram defended the Christian convert from the Kshatriyas who were stubborn and proud land lords. Often the missionaries protected converts with the help of the Government[7].

The history of conversions can be traced from the time of St. Xavier in 1536. Xavier converted entire caste of Bharats (Parvars) the fisher folk of the Coromandel Coast, perhaps 10,000 of them were baptised. Nobili between 1607-1602 converted 178 persons of higher caste[8]. Such movements in Tinnevally can be traced back to 1792 when large a numbers of Sharmars (Nadars) were radically mobilised and drawn into Christianity. Sometimes, the whole village was transformed and mainly the caste converts took the lead[9].

In the Telugu speaking region Christian missions used several effective methods to reach Hindus for conversion. For instance Education, Health and Famine relief works were the most important agencies for the mass movements.

The Church started an elementary school almost in every village congregation with the aim to make the Christians sufficiently literate to be able to read the Bible and to take interest in general affairs[10]. The village schools were rapidly developed Dr. Ferguson in this connection reported that "generally speaking in those villages where the maintenance of the school rests with the teacher and village community, the best result is obtained[11]". The work in schools were divided into the main departments of religion, secular, teaching, music and industrial instruction.

In secular schools they taught subjects like Arithmetic, geography, Bible etc., in schools at Ongole, Kavali, Podili, Narasarao Pet, Samalkot, Nandyal and Kalaspet. The elementary village schools especially in Machilipatnam and Eluru districts were also an extremely important factor in the spread of Christianity. In 1860's -1870's the Malas in particular, deprived of educated opportunities in the traditional system and stirred up by direct contact with christian preaching moved towards these schools. Teacher training by the missions enabled an effective system of education and instruction[12].

Prior to 1833, established elementary schools, teaching through the medium of Indian languages formed bulk of Christian education enterprise. In the period of 1833-57 in the high school and colleges the teaching emphasis was on the English language. The missionaries thought because of the western knowledge, science and technology, Hindus may be attracted to Christianity[13]. Prior to 1854 the christian missionary schools were run by societies from abroad. The great Despatch of 1854 is often called as charter of Indian education which gave aid for the schools especially for missionary schools run with the government Grant-in Aid funds[14].

In 1831 the American Lutheran Church mission maintained 1044 schools connected with 1566 congregations. In a large proportion, the mission day schools connected with the mass movements, employed only one teacher. The Andhra United Lutheran mission employees 1513 teachers for 1041 schools. The Church Missionary Society maintained 780 schools with 1076 teachers within the congregations in Krishna and Godavari districts[15]. The American Baptist, Canadian Baptise mission, the London missionary society, the Arcot missionary society and also other missionary societies had networks of village schools in the Telugu districts[16].

The Guntur and Rajahmundry Lutheran Mission established boarding schools in its surroundings, which were more helpful in providing more localized opportunity for village people to advance beyond the elementary village education. Such schools were started in Sattenapally, Narasaraopeta, Chirala, Tenali, Bheemavaram, Peddapur and Parvatipuram. Several of these schools advanced until they became high schools. The school in Pedapur, started by Dr.Edman in 1891 as a primary school, had a fourth form added in 1899 under the direction of the Rev. Hans Isaacson[17]. By April 1900 it became a high school. A new school was started by Rev. F.J. Mc Cready in 1908 in Rajahmundry. This was the only mission high school in the Rajahmundry field until 1916[18]. The Rev. Ernest Neudoerffer established a school and hostel in Bhimavaram in 1912. By 1914 it introduced a secondary section and raising it to the high school level in 1916.

The most outstanding institution was the Guntur Lutheran mission high school, which had been organised by Dr. Uhl in 1874. The Rev. Luther B.Wolf came to India in 1883 and raised the school to a second grade college affiliated to Madras University in 1885. It was named American Evangelical Lutheran mission college. In 1890 it started with 19 students. In 1903 there were 64 students enrolled[19].

The Rev. Roy stock became the principal. College classes were held with 211 students in 1914. Dr. stock was also incharge of Guntur High school, the middle school and the four branches of elementary school located in various parts of Guntur. In 1920 there were 160 students in the classes of the college, 279 in high school, 397 in the middle school. The four branches of elementary school had a total of 407 students in five classes. This made a grand total of 1241 in the institution. There were 71 teachers [20].

In 1941, the Hermanns berg mission had developed in addition to its village school, one high school at Tirupati, there middle school at chandragiri, Puttur, Nayudupeta, four girls high school at Tirupati, Gutur, Sullurpet and puttur. The high school at Tirupati gained an outstanding reputation after 1907, especially during the time of Rev. W. wickert, 1910-1915. statistics for 1915 reveal that there were 136 teachers and a total of 2. 866 students in Hermenns berg mission schools [21]. The schools and literary rate especially in protestant missionary schools in Andhra in Madras presidency was as follows:[22]

Year ....No Educated

1870 138

1880 440

1890 1,473

1900 3,500

1905 5,275

1910 6,099

1912 6,559

Missionaries were also the pioneers of women's education. Upto 1858, missionary work was primarily regarded as men's work. Between 1858 and 1908, the number of women engaged in the mission especially the wives of the missionaries increased. Special missionary societies were organised for women. The Zenana Bible and medical mission group set out a body with the title "The India female normal school and institution society". The Church of England Zenana missionary society was formed in

1880[23]. Zenana was defined by Drach and Kudler Zenana is used by the Hindus to designate the post part of the house, particularly among the wealthy classes which is assigned to the female members of the household wives, mothers and daughters of the Hindu families. It was a place no stranger or no man could enter[24].

The first Zenana missionary to arrive at Guntur was Miss. Kate Boggs with the Rev. Mrs. Schnure in 1881. In 1883 Miss. Anna S.Kugler and Miss. Fannie Dryden came to assist Mrs. unangst P.Lucy in zenana work[2]. Mrs. Unangst and Mrs. Schnure opened the Hindu girls school in 1883 in Guntur and Mangalagiri. These women urged Christians to educate their daughters. They appealed to Hindu and Muslims as well. The missions started school in four villages in Guntur area 65 percent of Christian boys and only[22] percent of the girls attended the local missions schools. The first organised mission work for Muslim women and children, began in February 1884 in Chinna bazar in Guntur. The work among Muslim women was started by Mrs. Unangst, Dr.Kugler also gave medical treatment at their home27. A school opened for Muslim girls in 1884 Mrs. Jane Rallier was the first single woman to learn Urdu. She worked among Muslim women upto 1903. Mrs. Jessie Thomas was assigned to work in 1908. Miss. Thomas had six girls who knew urdu and who worked with her as teachers and zenana workers[28].

In the schools of Vidya nagar area, in Krishna District, girls formed 39. 9 percent of the enrollment in the 1st standards and only 10.9 percent in other standards. Speaking of Guntur schools statistics show that girls formed 39.9 percent in the 1st standard and 22 percent in the other standards by 1926. The percentage of girls in the schools was 14.8 percent in Vidyanagar, and in Guntur it was 13.9 percent29. In 1885 it was decided by the Lutheran mission conference to educate woman in the congregation. In 1926 over 300 organizations were working among the converts for women. More than 36,700 were baptised and 5,500 could read the Bible30. The church missionary society gives the record about schools in Krishna and west Godavari districts for 1926 and 1931[31].

Year	No. of Schools	No.of Teachers	Christian	Non-Christian
1926	635	1031	10454	10954
1931	780	1076	11708	10020

source: pickett, The Christian mass Movements in India, p.281.

A large proportion of missionary schools had only one teacher. The Andhra United Lutheran mission employed 1,513 teachers for 1,041 schools (These figures do not include the college, high school and Bible Training schools). The church mission society reported that by 1931 the Krishna and West Godavari districts recorded 780 village schools with 1076 teachers[32]. The one teacher schools were at Cumbum 5 to 10, at Guntur 11 to 15, Vidyanagar 6 to 12.

Mrs. william J.Ccutter opened the first girls school at Rajahmundry in 1852. In 1882, Mrs Schmidt stared a school for girls. The first zenana work began at Narsapuram. A district munsiff permitted his wife and daughter with five other members to be taught by Mrs Schmidt and Mrs.Artman. Artman continued with her work in 1890. Miss Agnes schade and Miss katherine Sadler arrived in Rajahmundry in 1891 Mrs Schade started a Hindu girls schools. She showed a great deal of interest in educational field so that there came to be so many schools run by Rajahmundry mission.

More woman missionaries arrived as the work expanded. New Hindu girls schools were established in different parts of Rajahmundry and its outskirts. Miss Charlotte Swenson who arrived in 1906 that 270 home were visited weekly and 1200 women and children were under instruction. At the close of this period, in addition to the central girls school in Rajahmundry conducted by Miss Schade, Boarding schools were established in Samalkot and Bhimavaram in 1918-1919[35]. In 1920 twenty two women came to Rajahmundry to serve in Zanana and medical work.

In the Hermannsburg Mission field, a girls school was established in 1869, with a connected boarding school at Gudur. After, the school was transferred to Kodur, where Mrs. Woerrlein, who had an excellent Knowledge of Telugu, developed the school and widened its activity. When Woerrlien become mission director, he made Gudur his head quarters in 1892, and the girls school was transferred once more to that centre36. At first, this school was mostly for orphans and unwanted girls. The child ding were trained in cleanliness, orderliness and industry as well as regular school subjects. Home making was taught to the girls. The profit from the sale of Lace which was sold in Germany and America helped to support the school. Many of these girls became wives of native Christian workers. Woerrlein's daughter, Magdalene became the first Zenana worker on July 23,1901 .At the end of the first year, Mrs Woerlien and her daughter were busy visiting Hindu and Muslim homes in Gudur. They were assisted by Rachel, the widow of a catechist, who had been teaching in the girls boarding school.

Miss Adele Schickinz arrived in 1904 to take over the work from Mrs. Woerrlein and her daughter, The work expanded. A native teacher was employed for the fancy lace work. A school was built and completed in 1906, and Miss Martha Woerlein came in the next year to take the charge of the lace school. This relieved Miss Schichinz for full Zenana work. A new zenana station was opened in Tirupati in 1908. Miss Schiekeinz moved there when she was replaced in gudur by Miss Marthadrews. The first baptism in Tirupati through Zenana work was the wife of the police Inspector, on July 17,1910. In the next year 24 were baptized at Gudur.

Miss Schickinz married a missionary Linder in 1921, but continued in the work as her husband was located at Tirupati. In the same year two deaconesses came out India to enter the work. Elsie Kastens and Anna Marie Meyberg. The work expanded in the next few years to Puttur, where Manekes wife supervised the work of two Bible women and two women teachers, one in the middle school and one in the middle school and one in the elementary school. Sister Elsie opened a new work in Venkatagiri in 1914. She visited Raja's wife and, found her illiterate. More Zanana women were ready to come from Germany for zenana work when the war brokeout.

A Widow's home had been opened by Mrs. Scribe in Kalahasi in 1908, but this was closed during the war. Another interesting feature of the women's work was the first women's conference held in Gudur under Mrs Woerrlienis direction, on March 3, 1909. Subjects for discussion were the place of women in the homes (Christian and Hindu), the visitation of sick, the teaching of the uneducated and the improvement of home living. Local women samajs (societies) were recommended with one of its activities to be sewing so that clothing could be prepared for the poor children. Before the war, the zenana work in the Hermansburg mission focused on 80 homes which were being contacted weekly with activities centering around hand work, bible stories and hymn singing. Some were instructed in reading, The workers also visited many christian women in their homes regularly[37].

Like educational work, the medical missionaries occupied an outstanding position in Christian missionary activity. The first mission to adopt a regular policy of sending medical missionaries to India was the American Board. The first medical evangelist in South India was John Scuder, who arrived at Madras in 1836[38]. Medical missions were neglected by foreign mission board because of the financial situation and also they never considered medical work as a means of Evangelization up to the middle of the 19th century. But in the later period, missions began to give more attention to medical work. The medical Evangelists who took their medical chests out to villages, combined medical treatments with the preaching of the Gospel. This led the missionaries to take resolution in South Indian missionary conferences held at Ooty and subsequent similar conferences to increase medical missionaries. Keeping these objectives in mind, the Lutheran mission had set up hospitals, dispensaries and nurse training schools in different parts of Guntur and its surrounding in Krishna district. These included the hospital in Guntur 1899, the hospital in Chirala in 1903, at Tenali in 1912, and the hospital at Rentahintala in 1814. Besides these, dispensaries were also opened at Tenali in 1908, Durgi and Tarlapudi in due courses. To cater to the needs of these hospitals nurses training schools were opened at Guntur in 1899, Rentachintala in 1922 and Chirala in 1927[39].

The medical work of the Andhra Lutheran mission was begun by its founder Fr.Heyer, He continued his medical work throughout his missionary career in Guntur, Rajahmundry and Palandu. One growth of lady missionaries and their helpers visiting women was that it brought to light the special need of women for medical work.

Anna Sarah Kugler (1883-1930) was the first medical missionary to start work at the Guntur hospital. In 1899 with the construction of a permanent hospital, she started her medical work with regular religious teaching. She perceptively saw the potential of medical work. She wrote "The hospital will afford opportunity for christian work that will make it one of the most powerful evangelistic agencies of the present day efforts of foreign missions"[40]. In the first twenty five years the hospital served 25, 531 patients. 9,677 were private in patients. One fourth were Christians, 19% were Brahmins, 34 percent Sudras and rest of other castes and out castes. In this work several Bible women were constantly employed at the hospitals to visit all the patients and tell Bible stories in the wards[41].

The next renowned lady medical missionary was Dr. Bear (1895-9142). She too had a share in the medical work of Lutheran Church in Guntur district during the furlough of Kugler. She carried the medical work with distinction and contributed for the growth of medical work with in Guntur district in general, and Chirala in particularly Dr. Bear's dispensary opened in 1906 at Chirala. Up to 1924, 5,300 patients were treated. Rentachintala hospital was opened in 1914. Dispensaries were also started at Turlapudi in Durgi, Nidadavolu, treated in these mission hospital were 48,950 by 1924. Dr.Alfred Pfitsh the man doctor, took charge of the newly opened Rentachintala hospital in may 1918. Since medical work required trained doctors, nurses and compounders, all medical missions were obliged to make some arrangement for training formed classes of the available people, generally Christians from mission orphanage and boarding schools and taught them in their own hospitals. In 1924 hospital staff included Kugler, two Indian medical graduates from Vellore medical school, and two missionary Indian nurses. The Guntur nursing schools were started in 1899 under the supervision of the Ms. Katherine Fahs from which over fifty Indian and Anglican nurses graduated. Another nursing schools was set at Rentaccchintala in 1992 and Chirala in 1927[45]. The Rajahmundry Lutheran mission medical missionary

Lydia Woener M.D. opened a dispensary in 1911. She reported a total of 2,026 patients 432 visits to home and 84 surgical operations at the end of first year[46]. The first missionary nurse was Ms. Head Wigwahlberg who came in 1902. A training school in Telugu for nurses, was started in 1918 under the direction of Ms. Anna Rohre and Hilma Levine, who came to India in 1915. Since 1912 Dr. Betty A. Neilson reported in 1924 as many as 1,317 in-patients were treated and 7,800 patients at dispensaries[47]. The Rev. Nicholas Witman (1896), a missionary of the Hermannsberg mission started as Asylum in 1905 in Kodur Witman not only served the Asylum with his additional knowledge of medicine, but he also set up a clinic and treated about 3,000 individuals in the course of the first year. About the same time, the Schleswig Holsteiun mission established a leper Asylum at Salur with financial assistance from America. It was called "Philadelphia Leper Home[48]. In 1926 Protestant mission hospitals numbered 55. They however decreased to 38 in 1930 -34 they shot upto 67 in Andhra.

The Hermannsberg mission medical work created a friendly attitude on the part of the Andhra population. Medical missionaries treated both Christians and other castes in a secular way. After a while the proselytising effort took a secondary role to medical and health care[49].

Industrial work became another important part of the education because the mass movements, resulted in lots of sudras and low castes leaving their caste occupation for betterment of their social status. The industrial work training was seen as the best way to self-support[50].

Another important area of mission work was the imparting of technical training and education, Instruction in making lace, crochet edging and woolen caps grass and rope mats. Webbing for beds, Duries, bed chicks, Macaroni and Vermacilli, plain needle work dress making, Kalankare work, and drawn thread work was also taught[51].

Some of the prominent industrial schools were Coles Ackerman memorial school (American Mission), which was an Agricultural school at Nellore. A boarding school for 100 girls of the depressed classes drawn from villages of the Kurnool and Cuddapah districts was constructed by the Holly cross mission at Nandyal. At the latter institution instruction to prepare pupils as hospital nurses and mid-wives was provided. The S.P.G. mission of Gidalore (Cumbum Taluq) had a Higher Elementary vernacular school intended for Christians of the Church of England in Kurnool and Cuddapah districts[52].

Institutions of mercy conducted by the Guntur and Rajahmundry missions by 1920 was the Dorcas home for widows, deserted wives, crippled women and children, young girls needing protection and children was started in Samalkot and later moved to Rajahmundry and made a part of the industrial home. The orphanage in Guntur was constructed in 1904 to take care of orphans from Pandit Ramabai's home in Poona after the tragic famine of 1900. And a school for the blind was established in Rentachintala in 1911. The industrial working Guntur grew out of the orphanage. Efforts were made to teach the orphan boys cooking, carpentry, tailoring, weaving, motor driving as well as school teaching. The orphanage was closed in 1926 but the two main training institutions the carpenters shop and the printing press continued[53].

Mrs. George Albrecht opened a school for the blind in Rentachinthala in 1911. The braille system was adapted to Telugu, and in 1915 the school was recognised by the government and started to receive aid. Children joined from all over the Telugu area. A full curriculum in six standards according to government requirements was provided and in the industrial section crafts taught were rope making, tape making mats, cloth and basket weaving. For Christians of the church of England in Kurnool and Cuddapah districts, manual training formed a part of the educational curriculum. On the manual training side carpentry, weaving, leather work and agriculture were taught in the school. In Guntur district alone by 1937, there were United Lutheran mission Rural reconstruction school, the American mission cabinet-making industrial school and St.Joseph's industrial school for girls[54].

While educational work and medical care and facilities made the Church and conversion more attractive, it was the economic crisis of famines which really gave an impetus to conversions.

A critical role in conversion was famine relief works. There was a serious famine in the Telugu country in 1877-78 Rev. Rowe undertook relief operation with the relief committee of Madras. As a result, the relief operations attracted many hundreds into the church. Seventeen hundred persons were baptised during the two years following the famine. However, at the close of 1880, the Guntur Lutheran mission had grown to 5,423, nearly double the membership of 2,845 in 1875[31]. The Canadian Baptists baptised 119 persons in 1879 in the Cocanada, Tuni Cyclone[32]. The Baptist missionary Rev. Clough at Ongole undertook, the construction of Buckingham canal project at Rajaupalem and provided employment to nearly 3,000 people during famine in 1877-78 and several converted[57]. The Famines of 77-78, effected 30,000 children who sought industrial training[58].

In Telugu speaking area several missionary societies had in their fields drawn a good numbers of converts from the middle of the 19th century. In 1850, the areas like Nellore, Cuddapah and Kurnool contained 120 protestant Christians. Buy 1861 there were 3335 and ten years later they had multiplied to a large number of 13,798[59]. It is significant that most of the converts were from the lower castes and not from upper castes.

The mass-movements occurred in 1853 in Cuddapah. Two headmen instructed into the main doctrine of the Christian faith, helped missionaries to convert a 100 malas in Cuddapah and also 274 persons belonging to the neighboring village[60]. The conversions grew rapidly Statistics show that the adherents in 1861 were 1250, in 1871 it was 2793, and in 1881 it was 6331, forming no less than 90 congregations in the various villages of the Cuddapah district[61]. Rev.R. Johnston of L.M.S Schicacole started work in Nandyal. At the end of the 1861 this mission had 236 converts, and in 10 years more than 939. But in the year 1881 the entire mission rose to 2,900. Thus Cuddapah and Nandyal had a christian community of 9,231 native Christians by 1885[62].

In the initial stage of Evangelical work, Rev. Darling the C.M.S. missionary who visited Raghavapuram at the request of Venkaiah made a center for his mission[63]. It was with Pogali Venkaiah a notorious rober with whom the Telugu mass-movement was born in March, 1859, as Darling baptised Pogalu Venkaiah, together with the fifteen others. With in twelve years Venkayya himself had converted 70 souls. When he became a christian, the converts of the church missionary society numbered 200, most of them were not Telugus, When the died in 1891, after 32 years of continual efforts, the number of converts were 10,000. Venkayya's conversion covered a whole village and from these the gospel spread to 13 villages[65]. The sons of students of the missionary schools and especially women were baptised.

The above concessions highlight first the method of converting a village head man or a family head first, who could then influence his village people and relatives to convert. The missionaries always used this method of first converting an influential head of the village or head of the family. In the year 1884, 41 people were baptised in Tallada, 27 in Singaraya Palem and 51 in Gapavaram, Komatlagudem had 4 converts in 1885, 41 in Muddanaur, 21 in Burda Raghavapuram, 10 in Khammam[66]. Rev. Harrison a C.M.S. missionary who worked in Bezawada for 41 years came to the Eastern part of Khammam and preached and won many souls for Christianity in Sundrapatla, Rolupadi and Lankapalli[67.] In 1888 Mr. and Mrs. Panes, C.M.S. missionaries, took up their head quarters in Khammam with a centre under their care. This centre contained 24 villages in which there were 365 Christians and 83 enquirers[68].

The first Baptist conversions was from Thalakondapdu, Kanigiri taluka near Ongole. Yerrakuntala Perriah was a spiritual pioneer in Telugu land. In the churches around Nellore the majority of Christians were Madigas[69] Rev. Clough organised the church in Ongole in 1867. Under his long work 2,222 people were baptised in one day in the Gundalakamma river of Ongole, most of them from the Madiga community . This marked the beginning of the mass movement from the Madiga community into the Baptist churches of this area.

By 1869, 500 converts were noted in Ongole as well 55 converts were added at Nellore. In 1872 the whole mission consisted of 2,242. In 1876-77 a severe famine visited Ongole. As mentioned earlier Rev. Clough took a contract from government to construct the Buckingham canal, which gave a employment for six months to many thousand of people, During the later half of the June 1878, he baptised 1168 persons, in July 7513, and by the end of the year 9606 These additions made the membership of the Ongole church 12,804. 19,367 is given as number of communicants connected with Ongole and its out stations in 1881, and this represents a population of 50,000. At nellore the communicants were 454 and at Ramapatnam 531, with an aggregate of more than 3,200 nominal Christians[70].

Statistics are given below for the three stations of the mission existing in 1882 (Ongole, Nellore, Ramapatnam) :

American Missionaries   10

Ordained Native Preachers   46

Un-Ordained Preachers   249

Students Training for Christian Work   200

Church Members   20,757

Christian Adherents, Established   53,000

Villages in which Christians Reside, more than   600

Source : The Missionary Conference, South India and Ceylone, Vol-II. p.23.

The above table gives us the very rapid pace of christian conversions.

In Machilipatnam Mr. Fox and Nobiuli started education work. Mr.Thomas Darling came to work with Mr.Fox they together went from to place to place preaching and visiting places like Kankpadu, Bontumalli, Mylavaram, Rajadummuguda but gained only three converts[71]. Nobili started his work by opening a school at Machilipatnaam. His continued work enabled him to win only nine converts, one from Sudra community and one from Brahmin community after seven years. Nobili made his sincere effort to win high caste converts[72].

The work of the church missionary societies was greatly encouraged by the conversion as mentioned earlier of Gopal Venkaiah a fifty year old Mala. His conversion started a mass movement among his caste people. Later Madigas also became Christians in the Anglican church in the Krishna Godavari area[73]. The Society for propagation for Gospel, sent W.W. Wilport to Anglican church in Cuddapah. He stayed there for seven years touring Cuddapah and Kurnool districts. The conversion of Akula Nancharaiah a Mala started a mass movement of the Malas into the church[74].

One observes in Kurnool district very few Madigas becoming Christians as a result of the work of the societies for the propagation of the gospel and London missionary society. It was only after Dr.John E.Clough. a Baptist missionary from Ongole with Rev. D.H. Drake toured Kurnool districts in November 1875 that converts from Madigas came to be members in church[75]. The opening of a Baptist mission station at Kurnool in August 1876, encouraged the movement Madigas began to take a real interest in Christianity, because now they could become Christians without becoming a part of christian mission church in which Malas were in majority. It is significant to know that of the sixteen thousand Baptist Christians in West Kurnool districts are only a handful were converted from Mala community[76]. Two important factors influenced conversion. One was the conversion of a prominent leader or personality. His personal charisma facilitated mass conversion. The second important factor was there was different levels of status among the Mala the Madiga, connected with a wider rift in village relations, by which the population had been divided into the right hand and left hand caste[77]. This had a clear out influence on the mass movements, and the churches into which they converted.

The work in villages began by the Wesleyans in 1882, with the longer tour of the pioneers Burgess, Wesley and Benzman and Prett toured Siddipet, Karimnagar, Medak, which were soon marked out as the mission centres. The Gospel was first preached to the caste people in the villages and to the weavers of the Karimnagar who had become Christians. In Kavali, Telugu Baptist Church comprised mostly of Madigas, the second Baptist church was mostly of Malas. In 1874 Canadian Baptist Mission was established in Telugu country at Cocanada[78]. Brother John Craigs, Canadian Baptist in his tour of Gunnanapudi, made fifty two new converts who where baptised, in Akividu eighty one members were baptised. The rapid development in the patter in the area for the first five years was reported as follows[79].

     1880 -   50
     1881 -   168
     1882 -   220
     1883 -   178
     1884 -   125

Total baptised were recorded as 1,118. The growth in and around Coconada field was as follows.

1880 -	41
1881 -	52
1882 -	40
1883 -	139
1884 -	106

Total congregations were twenty one in 1871. In 1875 a society had placed three missionaries at Chicacole, Bhimulipatnam and Bobbili in the Visakhapatnam District[80].

The Lutheran Mission was started in 1842 by Fr. Heyer with stations in Rajahmundry and Palnad. Heyer baptised thirty nine persons in 1884 in Palnad form low caste. In 1850 there were one sixty four Christians in both stations. By 1881 they had increased to three hundred and thirty eight, and at the end of 1871 the christian community had increased to two thousand one fifty, of whom six hundred were communicants, congregations were thirty two. These were connected to fifty two villages. In 1881, the adherents had increased to 7,988, the communicants to 2,404 the congregation to 120. The christian preachers and teacher to ninty five and the schools to 1965. These results were gratifying for a small mission established as recently as 1842[81].

At Rajahmundry, the American Evangelical Lutherans were successful, and at Guntur and Palnad in the Krishna district. In 1861 after fifteen years labour they had 29 Christians. At the close of the next ten years of labour the mission, could rejoice in 320 converts and 93 communicants, and by 1881, it had 707 adherents. 259 of them being communicants82. When Fr.Heyer left India in 1871 there were 240 baptised in Rajahmundry mission and the number was raised to 335. However, by the close of 1880 the baptised numbers in Guntur mission had grown to 5,423 nearly double the membership of 2,845 to 1926. The membership increased to 13,566 in 1890 to 18,964 in 1900. The number of villages in which church member lived increased from 362 to 529. In the Rajahmundry mission in 1990 the numbers had increased to 6159.

Aat the Kurnool mission stations Kalasapadu, Mutyalapadu and Nandyal the members were as follows.

Year	Congregation	Baptists	Catechumens
1879	78	2377	1795
1889	115	5582	2325

The progress in Mutyalapadu and Nandyal during 1889-1999   was as follows.

Year	Congregation	Baptists	Catechumens
1889	115	5562	2325
1899	172	9441	3360
1910	230	13541	5150

Source: Herbert Ware : The Telugu Mission, P.119,122

During the second half of the 19th century there was a rapid growth and expansion in conversion. In 1885 the total number of the protestant christian community was 91,092 but in 1900 it increased to 854,8867. This show the marked increase in conversions in second half of the 19th century. The grand total of the Indian christians in 1851 was 91,029. In the following decade it had grown to 138,731 (increasing of 47,639 or 15 percent) by 1871 it reached to 224,255 (an increase of 85,527 or 61 percent) In 1881 it stood at 417,372(an increase of 193,214 or 86 percent and four and half time as 1851)[83]. from 1891 to 1901 the Indian christians increased from 2,036,590 to 2,664,313 an increase of 30.8 percent while the whole population of Indian increased by only 2.5 percent. 1901 to 1911 christian population increased from 2,923,241 to 3,876,196. The census of 1901 gives us the total number of converts in krishna district. In 1881 the total number of christians were 36,194. A decade later the number increased to 68,524 (an increase of 32,330 or 89.3 percent). In 1901, the christian population stood at (101,414 an increase of 32,890 or two and half times or 180.2 percent as 1881)[84]. In the telugu country, in Madras presidency, according to census returns the number of chirstians rose from 19,131 in 1871 to 2,25,115 in 1801, an increase of over 2,03,000 in thirty years[85].

According to Rev.Alexander an CMS missionary in Eluru"the more general way for the spread of the movement is through friends and relatives,who do their best to bring over those belonging to them from distance places because the untouchable converts unlike those of high caste origin continued in the Hindu society.They were able to promote Christianity through continuing contact with friends and relatives for instance. Family gathering, weddings and even funerals were all occasions which facilitated the spread of Christianity[86]. Malas and Madigas travelling long distances in the normal course business, buying and selling skins or cotton cloth,.influenced others in the more remote parts of the county[87].

On the social causes of the mass movements Bishop White head of the Madras mission wrote in 1906 that the reason why large number of converts gathered in the church was almost universally the same powerful social cause, it was oppression of the land lords. The effect of the great famine, the tyranny of the Brahmins and other caste people over the poor,the pariahs, the desire for education and social advancement were motives for conversion. He argued that the chrisitan in contrast to a Hindu was the champion of the poor and oppressed. However, it was not only the poor who were becoming christians. The church itself refused to condone oppressions88. Converts at the end of the 19th century were mostly the from downtrodden classes of the society. It was perhaps due to their to escape from suppression, from caste oppression and also to benefit by the educational and social opportunities afforded by the church[89].

As stated above, one main reason for the spread of Christianity among the downtrodden castes was the faith that entrance to the church and also the new customs and traditions would enhance their status. The missionary who preached the message in regional languages which people were able to understand, appealed to them more than Hindu religion, with its pujas and rituals which were in Sanskrit, a language which the majority people could not understand.

The mass movements gathered momentum during the economic crisis like famines which resulted in extreme deprivations. It's true that he motives for conversion were not always religious.

Help in times of famine or epidemics, support against oppression by land lords and money lenders hope for better social standards, education for their children chances of employment in christian institutions all were powerfully contributory factors.

REFERENCES

1.　G.A. Goddi... **Christian Conversions in Telugu Country 1860-1900 : A Case Study of One Protestant Movement in the Godavari-Krishna Delta**, I.E.S.H.R., Vol.12, 1975, P-61.

2.　C.B. Firth... **An Introduction to Indian Church History**, C.L.S. Madras, 1980, P.193.

3.　Ibid.

4.　Stephen Neil.... **A History of Christian Missions**, Britain, 1984, P.187.

5.　R.E. Frekenberg... **The impact of Conversion and Social Reform upon Society in South India during the late Company period**, Cited in C.H. Phillips and Md. Waiwright (Eds), Indian Society and Beginnings of Modernisation, London, 1967, P.123.

6.　G.A. Oddie... **Christian Conversions in Telugu Country**, I.E.S.H.R., 1970, P.61, also M.L. Dolbeer... **A Hisotory of Luthernism in Andhra Deshaa - 1842-1900**, New York, 1959, P.61.

7.　Dolbeer... **History of Luthernism**, Op.Cit., P.213, Phillips... **Out Castes Hope**, London, 192, P.80.

8.　Stephen Neil, Op. Cit., P.149-187.

9.   Neil, Op.Cit., P.33,67, Fregkenberg... also **The impact of conversion**....Op., Cit., 123, Cadwell, **The Early History of the Tinnevally Mission**, Madras, 1881, P.70-78.

10.   Drach and Rudler... **The Telugu Mission of the General Council and EvangilicalLuthern Church America**, Philadalpha, 1914, P.12.

11.   White Head... **Our Policy in India**, Madras, 1907, P.28.

12.   G.A. Oddie... Op., Cit., P.73.

13.   Perumali H.C. and Hamby E.R (ed) **Christianity in India**, Allepphy, South India.

14.   G.A. Oddie... Op., Cit., P.73, and Picket, **The Christian Mass Movements in India**, Lucknow, 1933, P.282.

15.   Picket..op., cit., p-281.

16.   Ibid., P.278

17.   Dolbeer M.L.... **Andhra Evangelical Lutheran Church Brief History**, Rajahmundry, 1950, P.3, c.f. Dolbeer **History of Luthernism**... P.323.

18.   Ibid., P.324

19.   Ibid., P.328

20.   Dolbeer...**A.E.L.C. Brief History**,P23, 43, 52-54, and also Swavely... **One Hundred Years in Andhra Company**, Madras, 1942, P.47,56, Dolbeer... **Luthernism in Andhra**, P.326.

21. Haceius... **Hermnnansbergh MissionBlat**, 1910, P.342-43, cited in Dolbeer Luthernism in Andhra, P.327.

22. **Minutes of Andhra Christian Council**, Madras, 1933, P.38.

23. Picket.... Op., Cit., P.278

24. Neil Stephen... **The Story of Christian Church in India and Pakistan**,C.L.S., Madras, 1922, P.105.

25. Drach and Kudler... Op., Cit., P.270, and Dolbeer **History of Luthernism**, Op., Cit., P.315, also Perumalil and Hamby (ed) **Christianity in India**, Op., Cit., P.274.

26. Dolbeer... **A History of Luthernism**, Op., Cit., P.163

27. Picket... Op., Cit., P.287

28. Ibid., and Swavely, Op., Cit., P.262-266.

29. Dolbeer... **A Brief History of Luthernism**, Op., Cit., P.

30. Picket, Op, Cit., P.288.

31. Ibid., P.281

32. Ibid., P.285

33. Dolbeer... **Luthernism in Andhra**, P.320.

34. Wolf, **After Fifty Years**, P.196, also see Swarely, **One Hundred Years**, P.254, Dolbeer, **A.E.L.C. Brief History**, P.20-21, 43-44,Penumalil & Homby E.R. (Ed) **Christianity in India**, Op., Cit., P.274.

35. Drach, **Kingdom Path Finders**, Philadelphia, 1942, P.89-103, Swarely, **One Hundred Years**, P.269; Dolbeer, **A.E.L.C. Brief History**, P.33, 50-53, Drach & Kudler, Op., Cit., P.98, 205, 304, 310.

36. Devadas, **75 Samvatsaramlu Klupta Charitra** (Telugu), Madras, 1941, P.30-37, 39, 52, 54, cited in Dolbeer.

37. Ibid., P.30-37, 50-54

38. C.B. Firth, O.Cit., P.199.

39. Ibid., P.202

40. Dolbeer, Op., Cit., P.328

41. Brach, **Our Church Abroad**, 1926, P.62

42. Ibid., P.68

43. Ibid., P.67

44. Ibid., P.68; Dlbeer, Op., Cit., P.332

45. Dolbeer, Op., Cit., P.332

46. Ibid., P.336

47. **Minutes of the Third Meeting of Andhra Christian Council** (Medak), 1927, Appendi

48. **Minutes of 5th A.C.C.** (Guntur), 1931, Appendix

49. **Minutes of 7th A.C.C.** (Guntur), 1937, Appendix

50. **Bulletin of A.C.C.**, Guntur, 1923, P.31

51. **Report of the South India Missionary Conference** held at Madras, January 25, 1900, Madras, P.14, Also, **Reports of the Candadian Baptist Mission**, 1880, P.2.

52. **Baptist Magazine**, Bostan, Vol.65, 1880, P.2

53. Kesavanarayana, Op., Cit., P.186

54. Stephen Neil, **A History of Christian Missionary Great Britain**, 1964, P.149, 187.

55. M.A. Sherring, **Protestant Missions in India**, P.403

56. Ibid., P.404

57. Ibid., P.407

58. Ibid., P.408

59. David Downie, **The Lone Star**, Philadelphia, 1924, P.240, S.S. Subayya, Dornakal Dioces History S.P.C.K., 1939, P.136

60. Devadas, P.26, Gladstone, **The C.M.S. Telugu Mission**, Mysore, P.23

61. G. Mackenzie... **A Manual of the Krishna District in the Presidency of Madras**, Madras, 1883, P.375, and Gladstone, Op., Cit., P.14.

62. Subbbaya, Op., Cit., P.138.

63. Gladstone, **The C.M.S. Mission**, Mysore, P.23

64. Subayya, Op., Cit., P.16

65. M. Yesuratnam, **Triple Golden Jubilee of Church Missionary Soceity**,1949, P.5

66. B. Senzamin, **Andhra Pradesh Christian Church History**, 1976, P.48.

67. **Baptist Missionary Magazine**, Vol.65, No.12, Dec,1885, Bosten, P.6-7, 17; also V.R. Devadas, **An Examination of Caste in the Churches of Andhra Pradesh**.

68. A.T. Fishman, **For this purpose**, N.D; p.11-12

69. Ibid, P.43

70. V.R. Davadas, **An Examination of Caste**, P.24

71. Ibid., P.28, David Downie, **The Lone Star**, Philadalphia, 1924, P.245.

72. David Downie, op., Cit., P.248.

73. Ibid., P.240

74. Davadas, **An Examination of Caste**, P.26.

75. J.W. Picket, **Christian Mass Movement in India**, Lucknow, 1933, P.27, also V. Rama Krishna, **Social Reforms in Andhra**, P.49

76. Drach & Kuder, **The Telugu Mission, Philadalphia**, 1914, P.170

77. **Canadian Baptist MissionaryAnnual Reports**, 1884, P.34

78. Ibid., P.

79. W.G. Caarder, Beginnings of the Canadian Baptist Mission to India, **I.C.H.R.**, 1969, P.135.

80. G.A. Iddie, Christianity in the Hindu Cribile, contiuity and change, 1850-1900, **ICHR**, June, 1981, P.72.

81. Ibid., P.73

82. **Baptist Missionary Magazine**, Boaston, Vol.65, No.12, Dec, 1885, P.459.

83. Ritcher, Op., Cit., P.219 and also see G.A. Oddie, **Christian Conversion in Telugu Country**, P.61.

84. **Census of India**, 1901, P.48

85. G. Phillips, **Out Castes Hope**, London, 1912, P.80.

86. G.A. Oddie, Christianity in the Hindu Crubicle, **I.C.H.R.**, June, 1981, P.72

87. **Baptist Missionary Magazine**, Dec, 1885, Op., Cit., P.459.

88. Ibid.

89. White Head, **Our Policy in India**, Op., Cit., P.76.

CHAPTER-5
CONCLUSIONS

The study is devoted throughout to explore the ideology and methods of missionaries for the spread of Christianity. In Guntur and surroundings in Krishna District in 19th century.

Speaking of the Andhra, with specific reference to Guntur region, one finds, missionaries have left us with details of the varied activities in this area. A critical analysis of their work has been undertaken to discuss the motives and ideology of the missionaries and their contribution to different fields.

As far as the history of 19th century Christianity is concerned, one cannot clearly distinguish the political and religious objectives of the missionaries. There are Indians who argue that those who came from Britain were primarily motivated by political considerations. Brahm D. Bharathi, for example asserts, "As the conversion of the Hindus to Christianity was going to prove political advantageous to the English people, it happened to be the main motivation behind all the English efforts to convert the Hindus to Christianity[1]. He rejects altogether the missionaries claim to be guide by spiritual motives and insists that the real purpose behind their masquerades, was political. Similarly T.R.Vedamtham declares "It is a mistake to think that Christian missionary enterprise is a religious movement.

It was always politically motivated"2. Indeed some of the early missionaries maintained quite explicity on occasion that their activity was politically advantageous. As cited earlier the arguments put forth in England to change the Charted Act to allow missionaries in India quite unabashedly talked of the link between missionary work and the strengthening of the empire. The government tried to promote the interests of the missionaries especially from 1813 Charter Act, helped them by granting funds. The government officials also helped the missionaries in many ways. On the other hand, the missionaries by their various agencies like education, hospitals and famine relief works tried to incorporate the idea of Gospel in to the general public which in turn they believed would help in christianistion of India, and lead to the legitimisation of colonial rule in India.

Caste in Christianity is one of the major problems debated by the missionaries. Since Christianity spread in India missionaries had no special intentions to work with a certain group of people but they always looked forward to establish themselves with the native people. According to this study, one observes that, Roman catholic and also Protestant missionaries never had any special policies to deal with the caste distinctions in Christianity. Missionaries allowed the caste distinctions in church. With the available evidence one can observe two important reason, firstly, they had to establish themselves, therefore could not face any opposition from the natives and secondly they were for the first time exposed to the caste distinctions.

By the middle of the 19th century one can see a change in the attitude of majority of British and American missionaries who considered caste as an obstacle to the spread of their religion and also declared caste as a fundamental institution of Hinduism. This brings us to another major conclusion that missionaries were against retaining caste, because converts retained an important part of their former religion which contradicts the idea of equality implicit in Christianity.

The fight against caste distinction in Christianity became more problematic because of the sudden growth of mass - conversions to Christianity which were dominated by panchamas. This indirectly affected upper - caste Hindus who were not willing to convert for the fear that they would also be degraded to low caste in society. Caste figured prominently in the deliberations of the missions. Missionaries passed resolutions in the National level conference like 1850, Madras missionary etc., that the Church would fight against caste in general and within the church especially. There was, however, a wide gap between these public utterances and practice within the church.

However, despite the efforts of missionaries to convert large number of caste Hindus and untouchables from Guntur region in Andhra, they failed to eradicating their social level of caste consciousness though they believed in the church. Quite often the missionaries did not even succeed in eradicating the basic sub-caste distinctions between the Malas and Madigas.

This brings us to another major question that has been sought to be explained and that is how did these people of Christian faith try to convert uneducated rural people and convince them to better social and economic standing. One sees that this was done through various agencies. Since the beginning, conversions to Christianity by the Indian people were for different reasons but they changed from time to time. In 16th century, the Malabar coast fisher folk were converted to Christianity for the sake of gaining security from land lords when Portuguese missionaries promised them protection. But in Guntur it is totally different. When high castes converted, one cannot conclude on any sort of exact cause for their conversions especially when the higher castes were well established economically and socially. Therefore this form of conversion can be concluded as a spiritual one. There were several means, directly or indirectly through which the missionaries were able to address and ameliorate different problems, food for work and shelter during economic crisis, like famines, providing access to water, health care, better employment, settling of disputes, enabling the use of civil courts in favour of low caste converts and most importantly providing educational facilities of boarding, lodging and stipends.

In successive periods, conversions underwent rapid changes. To give an example in 19th century, missionaries adopted various innovative means and methods to convert. Especially the educational institutions were an effective media, starting schools in every congregational village and town. Their primary motive behind giving education to the converts and their children was to enable them to read the Bible. Missionaries attracted children and elders from all castes with their scientific instruments and schools for 3 children[3]. The missionaries emphasised on education, enlightenment and civilization as necessary preliminaries to direct Evangelism. Dr. Inglis, a Scottish missionary in India, believed that "little could be expected from mere preaching to an uneducated and barbarous people[4]. He emphasized the need to educate people. The educational work of missionaries raised hope and confidence in the people. The grant-in-aid system recommended by the Woods Dispatch of 1854, helped the missions to expand their educational work. In Guntur region, available evidence shows the rapid expansion in schools and particularly the efforts made in the direction of women's education.

The missionaries included the extension of welfare measures, particularly health care to the poor masses in deep distress caused by poverty or natural calamities. Support against oppression by landlords and moneylenders, hope for better social status and education often leads to conversion.

The missionary attack on the Hindu customs and social evils had an indirect influence on Andhra Social reformers. "Lenders such as Raghupathi Venkataratnam Naidu. Mutnuri Krishna Rao and Konda Venkatapaiah Panthulu came from he missionary institutions and were profoundly influenced by the ethical ideas, manners and conduct of Christian Missions. The social reform activities in relation to women and untouchables owed much to the influence of missionary teaching and inspiration of missionary work"[65].

While there is a wide measure of agreement among scholars concerning the passive role played by the Indian Christian community as a whole in Indian freedom struggle, there is also recognition of the fact that quite a number of Christians in particular the better educated supported it whole heartedly, by active involvement[6].

The influence of nationalism was manifested within the mission context by growing dissatisfaction with the reprehensiveness of foreign control over church. Perhaps the first formal expression of nationalist feeling within the Christian millieu was the near simultaneous attempts by several prominent Indian Christians in the late 19th century, to until Indian Christians into a self supporting and self-governing church[7]. A more successful expression of this new self-consciousness arose in the first decade of the 20th century with the creation of the national missionary society which, sought freedom from foreign domination and independence within the Indian church by utilizing indigenous personal founds for its evangelistic work[8]. Nationalism was drawing the Indian community together as a unity against the foreigners. It also influenced Indian Christians to come together[9].

To asses the place of missionaries in the Indian sub-continent and their role in strengthening the base of the British Government, it would be pertinent hereto quote Sir Rivers Thompson, Lieutenant Governor of Bengal, "In my judgement Christian Missionaries have done more real and lasting good to the people of India that all the other agencies combined. By their pure, unselfish lives, by the self sacrificing sympathy with distress and sorrow, by their living with the people and for the people, they have exercised a power and produced results that words cannot fully set forth they have been the salt of the country and the true saviours of the empire[10].

By the end of the 19th century and early 20th century missionary activity in some sense got separated from the colonial interests and acquired a different status. Missionary enterprise in the fields of health and education laid the foundations for modern health care and education in modern India.

In Guntur their work and activities among the lower castes were left an indelible mark to this day. The present day social consciousness and educational advancement among these classes in the result of the sustained educational work of the missionaries from the 19th century.

REFERENCES

1. Brahman, D. Bharathi, Political roots of Christianity in India, **Manthan**, Vol.4, No.3, May, 1982, P.86 cited in J.H. Proctor, Scottish missionaries in India, An Inquiry into Motivation, South Asia, Vol.XVI, No.1, P.43.

2. Proctor, Scottish missionaries, Op. Cit., P.43.

3. **The Missionary**, February, 1849, P.49 cited in **Gospel Witness**, 1942 May, P.378, and also Life and Letters of Fr. Heyer Gospel Witness, June 1940, P.381.

4. D. Mackichen, **The Missionary Ideal in Scottish Churches**, London, P.113, also see George Smith, The Life and Life of the Alexanders Duff D.D. LL.D., Vol.1, London, 1971, P.34; Duncun B. Forreste, **The Christianity and early Indian Nationalism VI European Conference of Modern South Asian Studies**, 1978, P.2.

5. **Vivekavardhi**, Feb., P.9, Madras Native news paper report, Madras cited in B. Kesavanarayana **Social and Political Factors in Andhra**, 1`900-1956 (unpublished Ph.D. Thesis), Osmania University, Hyderabad, 1966.

6. E. Bhathy, **Religious Minorities and Secular State** in J.R. Chandra and M.M. Thomas (eds) **Religious Freedom**, Bangalore, 1942 and A.V. Thomas, **Christians in Secular**

India, Rutherford, 1974. Cited in Lionell Caplan, Class and Christianity in South India, **Modern Asian Studies**, Britain, 1980, P.652.

7.   E. Bagge, The First Independence movement among Indian Christians, **Indian Church History Review**, 1924, P.85-78.

8.   Thomas, **Christians in Secular India**, P.103.

9.   Ibid., Op.Cit., P.30-35.

10.   M.L. Dolbeer, **History of Lutheranism in Andhra Desa**, New York, 1959, P.95.

BIBLIOGRAPHY

OFFICIAL SOURCES :

A)   Census :

Census of the Madras Presidency, 1871, Vol.II, Madras, 1874.

Census of India, 1881, 1891, 1901, 1911.

B)   Gazetters :

Gazetter of India, 1854, 1904, 1981

Imperial Gazetteer of India, 1865-1887.

The Gazetteer of the Indian Union Country and People, Ministry of Information and Broadcasting, Faisalabad, 1983.

MISSIONARY SOURCES :

A)   Reports of the Conferences of Christian Missionaries Report of the American Baptist Missionary Union, (39th Report) July, 1853.

Proceedings of the South Indian Missionary Conference held at Gotacamund, S.I.M.C., 1858.

American Baptist Missionary Union Report with the Proceedings of the Annual Meeting held at New York (54th Report), May 21-22, 1868.

American Baptist Missionary Fifty Fifth Annual Report, July, 1869.

Report of the Canadian Mission, 1880.

Canadian Baptist Missionary Annual Report, 1884.

Report on the General Missionary Conference held at Allahabad, 1872-73, London, 1873.

Administrative Reports of the Madras Presidency, 1875-1907.

The Missionary Conference South Indian and Ceylone, 1879, Madras, 1880.

Report of the Second Decennial Missionary Conference held at Calcutta, 1882-83, Baptist Mission Press, Calcutta, P.883.

Report of the Third Decential Missionary Conference held at Bombay, 1892-93, Vol.I & II.

Education Society's Stream Press, Bombay, 1893.

Report of the South India Missionary Conference held at Madras, Jan 2-5, 1900, Madras, 1900.

B) **Letters :**

Life and Letters of Father Heyer's own Story (Gospel Witness).

Letters and Telegrams to Andhra Evangelical Lutheran Council, 1923-26.

C) **Minutes :**

The First Evangelical Lutheran Synod in India, 1853.

Minutes of Andhra Christian Councikl, 1926, 1927, 1931, 1933, 1937.

Minutes of the Madras Church Council, SIUC, 1937.

Minutes of the Telugu - Oriya Council of the Canadian Baptist Mission, 1941. Minutes of Madras Missionary Conference and other Documents on the subject of Caste, 1850. Minutes of the Madras Missionary, 1850.

JOURNALS :

A)   American Baptist Magazine, Vol.I, 1817.

Bulletin of Andhra Christian Councils, Boastan, Guntur, 1923.

Church Missionary Intelligencer

East & West

Gospel Witness

Harvest Field

Indian Church History Review

Indian Economic and Social History Review

Indian Evangelical Review

Missionary Magazine

Religion and Society

B) **Unpublished Thesis :**

Alagodi, S.D.L., The Concept of Mission as Reflected in Protestant Missionary Conference in India from 1825-1982. V.T.C. Bangalore Master of Theology, 1973.

David, G. The Evangelical work in the Karimnagar District of A.P. from 1870-1930 (Bachelor of Divinities), 1977, A.C.T.C., Rajahmundry.

Johnson, B.J. Christian Mass Movement work and its Administration (Bachelor Diploma in Theology), U.T.C., Bangalore, 1972.

Kantha Kumar, V.B. The Spread and Development of Luthernism, 1845-1875, B.D.-1, U.T.C., Bangalore.

Luther, N. The Integration of Church and Mission in the Indian Churches with Special Reference to the Andhra Evangelical Lutheran Church, B.D. 1965, U.T.C., Bangalore.

Scott, Roland, The Christian Impart on Hindu Caste System, M.D. U.T.C., Bangalore, 1938.

Trueman, B.H. Sher, A. Study of the Ongole Mass Movement of 1878 and its Impact on the Converts, Madras (Master of Theology, Bangalore, 1984).

Yesupadam, C. History of Christianity in Andhra, 1842-1981 (Master of Theology), 1981.

A)   **Books :**

Aberly, John, n Outline of Missions, Philadelphia, Muhlenberg Press, 1945.

Albangh Dana, Light in Indian's Hand, Valley Forge, Judson Press, 1963.

Anthony Kroot (Fr.) The History of Telugu Christians in Andhra Desa, London, 1700.

Araraiah, V.S. Indian and Christian Movement, 1935.

Brockway, K.N. & Marjorie Sykes, Unfinished Pilgrimage (The History of South Indian Schools) 1823-1973, C.L.S. Madras, 1973.

Broomley, E.B. They were men sent from God. Scripture Press, Bangalore, 1937.

Campbell, Christianity in India

Clouth, E.R. While Sewing Sndles, Fleming, H. Revell Co., New York, 1899.

David, D. The Lone Star, Philadelphia, 1924.

Devaraj, B.E. History of Christianity in India, 1876-78, Vol.I, London, 1978.

Dolbeer, M.L. Brief History of Andhra Evangelical Luthern Church, Church Publication, Rajahmundry, 1950.

Dolber, M.L. A History of Lutheranism in Andhra Desa, New York, 1959.

Drach George & Kuder F. Calvin, The Telugu Mission of the Evangelical Luthern Church in North America, Philadelphia, 1914.

Drach George, Our Church Abroad, 1928.

Duboi's Abbe J.A., The State of Christianity in India, New Delhi (Reprinting), 1977.

Dudley Raymond, The Growing Edge of the Church, New York, Agricultural Missions, Inc., 1951.

Dutt Romesh, The Economic History of India under the British Rule, Vol.I, Delhi, 1978.

Farquhar, J.N., Modern Religions Movements in India, Mac Millan, New York, 1915.

Author unknown, History of the Telugu Christians, Trichnopoly, 1910.

Firth, C.B. An Introduction to Indian Church History, C.L.S., Madras, 1961.

Fisherman, A.T. Cultural Change and the Unprivileged, C.L.S., Madras, 1941.

Fleming Daniel Johnson, Building with India, Missionary Education Movement, New York, 1922.

Forrestes B. Duncan, Caste and Christianity, London, 1980.

Frykenberg R.E. Guntur District 1788-1848, Oxdford Press, 1985.

Gandhi, M.E. Christian Missions, New Delhi, 1941.

Gibbs, M.E. The Angilican Church in India, 1600-1970, Delhi, 1972.

Glad Stone, F.F. The C.M.S. Telugu Mission (being a short account of the Hundred Years, 1841-1941), Mysore, 1941.

Glad Stone, F.F. South India, 1930.

Gobbin Herbert, At Grips, (Talks with the Telugus of South India), London Missionary Society, New Bridge Street, E.C., 1913.

Herbertware, G. Christian Missions in Telugu Country, S.P.G., 1912.

Hough, J.A. History Christianity in India, 4 Vols., 1839-45, Seeley.

Hough James, History of Christianity in India, London, 1945.

Hanpert Joseph, C. South Indian Mission, The Madhurai Catholic Mission from 1535-1835, Trichinopoly, 1937.

Ingham, Kenneth, Reformers in India, 1793-1833 (An account of the work of Christian Missions on behalf of social reform), Cambridge, 1956.

Kugler Anne, Guntur Mission Hospital, Philadelphia, W.M.S., U.L.C. in America, 1928.

Lamb Frederick, The Gospel and the Mala : The Story of the Hyderabad Wesleven Mission, Mysore, 1913.

Latourette, K.S. A History of the Expansion of Christianity (7 Vols.), U.S.A., 1937-45.

Leach, E.R. (Ed) Aspects of Caste in South India, Ceylon and North West Pakistan, Cambridge, 1969.

Lindell David, T. Lutheran Church in America, Board of World Missions, New York, 1965-66.

Majumdar, R.C. (Ed) British Paramountey in Indian Renaissance, The Historyand Culture of the Indian People, Bombay, 1963.

Mangamma, J. The Rate Schools of Godavari, Hyderabad, 1983.

Karshman, J.C. Life and Times of Carey, Marshman and Ward Embracing History of Sanpore Mission, 2 Vols., London, 1889.

Natarajan Nalini, Missionary among Khsins, New Delhi, 1977.

Neil Stephen, History of Christian Missions, Hmonds Worth, 1964.

Neil Stephen, Colonialism and Christian Missions, London, 1988.

Neil Stephen, The Story of Christian Church in India and Pakistan, C.L.S., Madras, 1972.

Oddie, G.A. Social Protest in India (British Missionaries and Social Reforms) 1850-1900, New Delhi, 1979.

Fercival, P. Land of Vedas, London, 1856.

Philipis, C.H., The East India Company 1784-1834, Manchester, 1940.

Philips, P.O. The Depressed Classes and Christianity, Madras, 1925.

Pickett, J. Waskon, Chrstian Mass Movements in India, Lucknow, 1933.

Pickett, et al Church Growth and Group Conversions, Lucknow, 1956.

Rao, P.R. History of Andhra, New Delhi, 1978.

Richer Julius, A History of Mission in India, Edenberg & London, 1908.

Sen Gupta, E.P. The Christian Missionaries in Bengal 1793-1833, Calcutta, 1971.

Sharrock, J.A. South Indian Missions, 1910, West Minister.

Sherring, M.A. The History of Protestant Missions in India, 1706-171, London, 1875.

Sundker Bengt, Church of South India, The Movement towards Union, 1900-1947, London, 1954.

Swavely, C.H. Biographical Record, U.L.C.M. and A.E.L. Church, Guntur, 1938.

Swavely, C.H. One Hundred Years in Andhra Country (1842-1942), Madras, 1942.

Swavely, C.H. The Lutheran Enterprise in India Madras, 1942.

Teylor W. A Memoir of the First Century of the Earliset Protestant Mission and Madras, Madras, 1847.

Thiekkadath Joseph, History of Christianity in India and Pakistan, George Allen & Urwinj Ltd., London, 1954.

Turner Fenal, P. The Foreign Misisons Convention at Washington, 1925, Fleming H. Revell Co., New York, 1925.

Yarghese Tlitus & Philips P.P. Glimpses of the History of Christianity in India, C.L.S., 1983.

Veerabhadra Rao, Education and learning under E.I.C., 1880-1920, Hyderabad, 1968.

Warren, M.A.C., Social History and Christian Mission, London, 1967.

Webster John, C.B. The Christian Community Change in the 19th Century North India, Delhi, 1976.

Williams, B. John, Research Studies in the Economic and Social Environment of the India Church, International Missionary Council at Tambaram, December, 1938.

Wilson Robert Smith, The Indirect Efforts of Christian Missions, London, 1928.

Wole, F.B. After Fifty years or Historical Sketch of the Guntur Mission of the Evengelical Luthern Church of the General symod in U.S.A., Philedelphia, L.P. Society, 1896.

Wolf, L.B. (Ed) Missionary Heroes of the Luthern Church, Philladelphia, 1911.

ARTICLES

Arulanatham, A.D. Caste and Christianity, I.C.Q.R., Vol.VI, No.3, 1893, P.15-24.

Baggo, K. The first Independence Movement among Indian Christians, ICHE, May, 1924, P.65-78.

Benney, G.L. The Social Problems of the Andhra Christian Community, Religion andSociety, September, 1953, P.42-50.

Bower, H. Castein Native Church, L.E.R., April, 1878.

Caplar Lionel, Class and Christianity in South India, M.A.S., Britain, 1980, P.645-877.

David, H.D. Social Background of Baseil Mission Christians, The Problem of Caste, I.C.H.R., Vol.18, 1984, P.141.

Forrester, D.B. Indian Christian Attitude to Caste in 19th Century, ICHR, 1975, P.131-147.

Forrester, D.B. The Christianity and Early Nationalism, VI, European Conference of S.A.S., 1976, P.1-15.

Frykenberg, Robert, E. The impart of conversion and social reform upon the Society in South India during the late company period in Ch. Phillips and M.B. Waiwrigt (Ed.) Indian Society and Beginnings of Modernism, London, 1967,P.187-243.

Garder, W.G. Beginning of Canadian Church Mission to India, ICMB, 1969, P.135.

Grave,H. The Breast Cloth Contraversy, the Caste Conciousness in South Travancore, I.E.S.H.R., Vol-V, June, 1986, P.30-42.

Manar C. James, Testing Barrier between Caste and out castes, G.A. Christian Conversion Telugu Country, A case study of one Protestant Mission in Godavari Krishna Delta, IFSHR, XII, 1975, P.61-79.

Oddie G.A. Christianity in the Hindu Crurible. Continuity and change in the Kaveri Delta, 1850-1990, ICHR, June, 1981.

Pillay, K.K. The impart of Christian Missionaries on the caste in South India during the 19th century, H.R.C., Vol.XL, 1970.

Proctor, J.H. Scottish Missionaries in India, An engiry into Motivation South Asia, Vol. No.1, 1991, P.43-61.

Rajagopal, P. Caste and its relations to the Church, I.E.R., Vol.IV, Jan, 1977.

Sharrock, J.A., Caste and Christianity, I.C.Q.R., Jan, 1894.

Swavely, C.H. Missionary to India, 184-45, Gospel Witness, May, 1940, 349-62.

Swavely, C.H. The first Furlough, 1846-47, Returns to Guntur, 1848, G.W., June, 1940, P.381-415.

Wilson Henry, S. Baseil Misison Industrial Enterprise in South Kanara and its impact between 1834 and 1919, ICHR, P.90-104.

ABBREVIATIONS

A.B.M. .... Andhra Baptist Mission

A.C.C. .... Andhra Christian Council

A.C.T.C. .... Andhra Christian Technological College
Secunderabad

A.E.L.C. .... Andhra Evangelical Lutheran Church

A.T.C. .... Andhra Technological College, Rajahmundry

C.B.M. .... Canadian Baptist Mission

C.S.I. .... Church of South India

C.M.S. .... Church Missionary Society

G.W. .... Gospel Witness

H.R.C. .... Histocial Records Commission

I.C.H.R. .... Indian Church History Review

I.C.Q.R. .... Indian Church Quarterly Review

I.E.R. .... Indian Evangelical Review

I.E.S.H.R. .... Indian Economic and Social History Review

L.M.S. .... London Missionary Society

H.A.S. .... Modern Asian Studies

R.S. .... Region and Society

S.I.U.C. .... South Indian United Church

U.T.C. .... United Technological College, Bangalore

I.C.Q.R. .... Indian Church Quarterly Review

I.E.R. .... Indian Evangilical Review

I.E.S.H.R. .... Indian Economic and Social History Review